THE MARCH UP COUNTRY

DATE DUE

D0905954

THE
MARCH
UP
COUNTRY

a translation of Xenophon's Anabasis

W . H . D .
R O U S E

ANN ARBOR PAPERBACKS
THE UNIVERSITY OF MICHIGAN PRESS

First edition as an Ann Arbor Paperback 1964
All rights reserved
ISBN 0-472-06095-3
First published by Thomas Nelson and Sons Ltd. 1947
Published in the United States of America by
The University of Michigan Press
Manufactured in the United States of America
Book design by George Lenox

1995   1994   1993   1992   12   11   10   9

ᴌᴦ

XENOPHON

The author of this famous book of adventure, the *Anabasis,*
or *The March Up Country,* was born in or about 431 B.C.,
when the Peloponnesian war began. He was brought up as
a country gentleman in the Attic deme or parish of Erchia
(modern Spata), on the east side of Pentelicos, 17–18 miles
from Athens, to which he made frequent visits. Horses and
dogs he loved all his life, and wrote books about them; he
also wrote of hunting, and domestic economy, using words
and idioms of old Attic speech just as Sir Walter Raleigh
spoke broad Devon all his days. In his youth he knew
Socrates, and later wrote a book of *Memorabilia,* or notes
about Socrates, in which we can still see how the great man
looked to ordinary people. Interested in politics and history,
he wrote of these in the *Hellenica,* and in his *Agesilaos* he
described the military career of one of his great heroes,
whose campaign in Asia he shared himself. But his grand
epic was the *Anabasis,* in which he narrated the story of
the march (401–399 B.C.) of the ten thousand Greeks from
Sardis to the gates of Babylon, and thence back to the
Greek coast of the Euxine Sea.

The world as the Greeks saw it consisted of a little group of peoples, who felt themselves (with all their provincial differences) quite distinct in spirit, surrounded by other and inferior peoples whom they called "barbarians" (a name derived from their speech, which seemed to the Greeks incoherent babble—the "babblers," so to speak). The distinctiveness of spirit, wherever it came from, was real; and it consisted chiefly of a love of freedom in both mind and body, and a hatred of violence and bodily torture. In this spirit they stood alone in the world, like a little garden of flowers in a jungle. And at the time of our story, 401 B.C., they had withstood alone, like ourselves, a concerted attack from two quarters, viz. from Persia in the east and from Carthage in the west: for from the east, in 490 B.C. at Marathon and 480 at Salamis, the hordes of the Persian king had been defeated and his fleets destroyed; and in the west, the invading hosts from Carthage had been annihilated at Himera in Sicily and at Cumai in Italy, Himera in the same year as the battle of Salamis, 480 B.C.

Since that time there had been civil war between the Athenian Empire, which had been victorious over the Persians, and her southern rivals, the Spartans or Peloponnesians, who were jealous of that empire. In this war the Spartans were victors, which accounts for the dangers left for Xenophon and his men after their march down country to the sea; there were thousands of Greek warriors in different places who had experience of war but not of peace, and so were apt for military adventure.

Cyros the Great was founder of the Persian Empire; and his story as told by Herodotos is like a fairy-tale. We read of him in the Bible, and there too we find an account of how he conquered Belshazzar, King of the Chaldeans, in Babylon; and, too, the story (Daniel v) of the king's feast and the inscription on the wall, MENE MENE TEKEL UPHARsin, "Thou art weighed in the balance and found wanting." Also in the book of Esther we find Ahasuerus, or Xerxes, and the story of his Queen Vashti.

The Persian crown had now passed from Dareios the Great (of Marathon days) and his son Xerxes (of Salamis days), through Artaxerxes and Darios Nothos, to the elder son of the last, Artaxerxes II, excluding the younger son, Cyros, who was now conspiring against his brother in order to obtain the throne. Such conspiracies were not uncommon, and indeed have been known in Turkey within living memory. Cyros was now satrap of most of Asia Minor, and had dealings with many of the Greek captains, who remained in various parts of the land with bodies of troops ready to serve any master who would pay them as mercenaries, not unlike the Swiss of later days in Europe. Cyros kept in touch with many of these captains, and commissioned them to collect men and await his instructions. Among them were Clearchos, a Lacedaimonian, and Proxenos, a friend of Xenophon, and Cheirisophos, a Spartan, and Menon of Thessaly, the same man who plays a part in one of Plato's dialogues.

Meanwhile Xenophon had been eagerly sharing in the intellectual life of the wonderful century (about 500–400 B.C.) that saw the production of the great harvest of dramatists and poets, historians and philosophers, in which were the best specimens of all the arts, including dancing and music, which ever appeared in the world. For Xenophon its chief charm was the spirit of free debate embodied in the person of Socrates. When Xenophon thought of going abroad Socrates told him to consult the oracle at Delphi (*Anabasis,* III, i), which he did; but there he merely asked "which of the gods he should sacrifice to, in order to have good fortune on his journey," without asking whether he should take that journey, as Socrates told him he ought to have done; yet as he had taken it for granted he should make the journey, he decided he had best go on with it. He had been invited to go by Proxenos, who was in Sardis at that time, and who promised Xenophon an introduction to Cyros, with a fair hope of handsome profit.

CYROS

Although Cyros was less than twenty-one years old, he had already made his mark as commander and ruler; he was indeed a very able man, and Xenophon gives anecdotes to show his character. He was then satrap or governor-general of nearly all Asia Minor. He had not told his Hellenic captains his real object, however, which was to dethrone his brother and become Great King himself. On various pretexts he began his march, and marched on, gaining his reinforcements as he went; and led them from Sardis (whence he set out) to the River Maiandros and the city of Colossai (to which place St. Paul later wrote the *Epistle to the Colossians*). Advancing through Lycaonia and Cappadocia, he crossed over Mount Tauros by the pass called the Cilician Gates, sending Menon another way, which made the Persian garrison think that their flank was turned.

Now the men had to be told the real object of the expedition. The men mutinied, and were won over only with great difficulty and with pay and princely promises. At Issos in Cilicia the ships of Cyros brought up some reinforcements, including Cheirisophos the Spartan with 700 men. They marched across country to the Euphrates, till they reached the Araxes, a tributary, and crossed it. They next passed through a desert (five days' march), which Xenophon calls Arabia, living on game, which was plentiful, but there was not one tree to be seen. They came now to a defile (The Gates) leading from Mesopotamia into Babylonian land.

Cyros now had 12,900 Hellenes and 100,000 of his own

countrymen. They did not expect the King to fight, but suddenly he appeared at Cunaxa, about 50 miles from Babylon. The right of Cyros's lines, consisting of the Hellenes under Clearchos, was on the Euphrates, Cyros in the centre, and Ariaios, a Persian, on the left. Clearchos charged straight ahead with shouts and the battle-song; the Persians whom they charged were affrighted, and fled without slaying a man. Cyros meanwhile was watching Artaxerxes in the centre, and with only 600 men (chiefly friends called his "table companions") he charged the King and his bodyguard of 6,000 cavalry. Crying "I see the man!" and riding at him Cyros gave him a slight wound; but at the same moment he himself was struck in the eye by a javelin, which killed him. Thus ended the expedition of Cyros (3rd September, 401 B.C.).

Now that Cyros was dead Clearchos offered to support Ariaios as king, but Ariaios, fearing the opposition of the Persians, proposed instead to lead the Hellenes back to their homeland—by no means an easy task, since the land they were in, though fertile, was crossed by the "Wall of Media" and four ship canals between the Tigris and the Euphrates. The Hellenes might easily have settled where they were, and become a threat to the Persian Empire from within, yet at first the Persians did nothing against them, except to sack the Hellenic camp and take all their provisions. They then sent Tissaphernes the Satrap to propose friendship, but really in order to compass their destruction, as the issue proved. Tissaphernes led them to Sittace, a little below Bagdad, drew them over the bridge by means of a trick into Media, and took them along the river for ten days, as far as the River Zab. Clearchos had a meeting with Tissaphernes, who seemed so friendly that Clearchos accepted an invitation to a further conference in the Persian lines. Four generals and twenty captains, with a small guard, went into the enemy's tent. All were

massacred (one first being sent back to the King for torture).
A single subaltern escaped and brought the news, saying
that the Persians were riding about and killing any they
met.

XENOPHON TAKES ACTION

Now Xenophon came on the scene. He was not really
a soldier, but what we might call a special reporter; and
had been (as already told) invited by Proxenos, a personal
friend, to go on the expedition with Cyros, where he might
hope to see something of the world. So he, a country gentleman with some fortune, came to Sardis with horses and
money, and marched up country with Proxenos. When
the treachery occurred he sought out an officer of Proxenos,
and persuaded him that their only chance of survival was
to fight. They at once went round and collected all the
officers they could find, held a meeting at which they elected
others, and made ready to retreat. We need not detail the
adventures, which Xenophon tells better himself. The
Greeks defended themselves in Nimrud (Nineveh) and
Mespila, ancient walled cities, then and now in ruins. Day
after day the Persians attacked with missiles, but feared
to fight bodily. Xenophon and his men took council how
they should act, and resolved to go northward through
the country of the Kurds into Armenia. The military
manœuvres they practised are interesting, and show up
the characters of the actors well. Their adventures on the
mountains and in the snow were wild enough, but at last
after many days they were in the Armenian plains, and
for the time being happy and comfortable. They rounded
the springs of the Tigris: the satrap Tiribazos gave them
leave to pass, but played them false, and the Hellenes, after
seizing his camp and spoils, got through a pass where he
meant to intercept them. There is no need to detail their
hardships and adventures, since they were now near the

end. As they were marching on they noticed a disturbance on a hill ahead, and Xenophon ran up to explore, and saw man after man rushing up and shouting, and when he came closer he heard the cry, "Sea! sea!"

They were among their own colonies at last, but of course as soon as the danger was removed they all began to quarrel among themselves. They were now at Trebizond, yet it was a whole year longer before the army was finally settled. They had to sail across the Black Sea, and then had still further adventures, which are instructive to us for the light they throw on methods of dealing with colonial states. Xenophon finally marched on land to Cerasûs, Cherrytown (whence Lucullus brought us the cherry in 73 B.C.). Then he reviewed the soldiers, who now numbered 8,600 men. Their booty was divided up, one-tenth being consecrated to Apollo and Diana of Ephesos. They passed the country of the Mossynoicoi, who lived in nests among the trees, and the Chalybes, who worked in iron, and then Xenophon seems to have contemplated taking Phasis or some savage city and setting up a colony there. This intention was checked by a seer, Silanos, who spread among the troops a garbled version of it because he had a fortune in money which he wanted to take home. He was negotiating for ships with Sinope. Meanwhile personal slanders went on, and the troops grumbled at his conduct on the march. So he held a general assembly,[1] and the grumblers spoke out their grievances, and were properly met as in Athenian courts; so as he says, "It was all right in the end." They sailed to Sinope, and resolved to try to win something to carry home. They wanted Xenophon to be their commander; but politics made him decline, and they were persuaded to choose Cheirisophos the Spartan, so as not to slight the paramount power of Sparta. But the men split up into groups; the rule of Cheirisophos ended in a week, and he died of fever.

[1] Athenian officials had to submit to a personal examination after holding office.

Now Xenophon's attention turned to Calpe, a convenient little harbour, where he stayed some time. But a new figure now appeared, Cleandros, Governor of Constantinople, who arrived at an unlucky moment and did mischief. Xenophon dealt successfully with this difficulty, using the greatest tact. Various Spartan officials and menials also kept meddling and marring every attempt at an orderly retreat; they intrigued also with Persian officers against the public interest. Xenophon decided to go home. He was urged to go back to the army again, which received him with joy. Eventually he accepted an offer from Seuthes, a Thracian chief, to join him. Seuthes gave him a barbaric feast, which is fully described, but did not keep his fine promises of pay.

But the Lacedaimonians, having just declared war against the Persian satraps Tissaphernes and Pharnabazos, sent their general Thibron into Asia. The remains of the Ten Thousand, some 6,000 men, set out to join him, and marched through the Troas. There Xenophon leaves them.

LATER DAYS

Three years later he was fighting again under King Agesilaos of Sparta, one of his heroes, whose life-story he wrote. Meanwhile there had been political ferment in Greece; Athens and Thebes had joined in on the Persian side, and so Xenophon, being on the side against Athens, and having returned with the Spartan king to Greece, took part in the battle of Coroneia, 394 B.C. So a decree of banishment was passed against him.

But the Lacedaimonians rewarded him with an estate at Scillos, about two miles from Olympia; and there he lived, enjoying excellent hunting and writing his books. He paid the offering long since vowed to Artemis at Ephesos; and was comforted because a stream flowing through his estate was named Selinûs, and a similar stream flowed by Ephesos, and, says Xenophon, like Shakespeare's Fluellen, "there is fish and cockles in both."

His banishment was revoked; and both his sons Gryllos and Diodoros fought in the cavalry for Athens at the Battle of Mantineia, 362 B.C., in which Gryllos was killed.

EXTANT MANUSCRIPTS

The best extant MSS. of the *Anabasis* are: Parisinus 1640, written in 1320, after an original of the ninth century; Parisinus 1641, of the fifteenth century; Vaticanus 987, later than the above; Etonensis, of the fifteenth century. Of these, the main MS. is Parisinus 1640, from which the others were copied. Other important MSS.: Bodleianus (lib. Canon, 39), of the fifteenth century; Vindobonensis 95, of the fifteenth century.

TRANSLATOR'S NOTE

Before me are three books that I have levied for notes, otherwise I have made my own translation: *Xenophon,* by Sir Alexander Grant (Blackwood, 1871); *The March of the Ten Thousand,* by H. G. Dakyns (Macmillan, 1890); *Travels in the Track of the Ten Thousand Greeks,* by William F. Ainsworth (John Parker, 1844).

CONTENTS

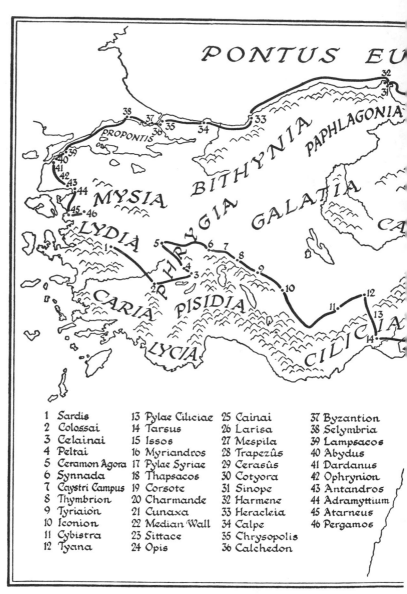

1 Sardis	13 Pylae Ciliciae	25 Cainai	37 Byzantion
2 Colossai	14 Tarsus	26 Larisa	38 Selymbria
3 Celainai	15 Issos	27 Mespila	39 Lampsacos
4 Peltai	16 Myriandros	28 Trapezûs	40 Abydus
5 Ceramon Agora	17 Pylae Syriae	29 Cerasûs	41 Dardanus
6 Synnada	18 Thapsacos	30 Cotyora	42 Ophrynion
7 Caystri Campus	19 Corsote	31 Sinope	43 Antandros
8 Thymbrion	20 Charmande	32 Harmene	44 Adramyttium
9 Tyriaion	21 Cunaxa	33 Heracleia	45 Atarneus
10 Iconion	22 Median Wall	34 Calpe	46 Pergamos
11 Cybistra	23 Sittace	35 Chrysopolis	
12 Tyana	24 Opis	36 Calchedon	

Route taken by the Greeks in their

march up country under Xenophon

BOOK ONE

~~~~~~

I

Dareios and Parysatis had two sons, the elder Artaxerxes,
the younger Cyros. When Dareios was ill and expected to
die, he wished both his sons to be present. The elder was
there, as it happened, but Cyros had to be sent for from
the province where he was governor and general-in-chief
over all the troops that are stationed in the plain of the
Castolos. Cyros then came up to the capital, taking with
him Tissaphernes as his friend, and he brought up 300
men-at-arms of the Hellenic mercenaries under their captain Xenias, a Parrhasian. But when Dareios died and
Artaxerxes succeeded, Tissaphernes slandered Cyros to his
brother and said he was plotting against him. The king believed him, and seized Cyros to put him to death, but his
mother begged him off and sent him back to his province.

When Cyros got clear of this danger and disgrace, he determined never again to be in his brother's power, but to
make himself king instead, if he could. Cyros had his
mother behind him to begin with, for she loved him more
than the reigning Artaxerxes. Whenever anyone came to

Cyros from the court, he treated them all so well that they went away friends to him rather than to the king. And the native troops he had he carefully trained to take the field, and made them loyal to himself. Hellenic mercenaries again he assembled in as great force as possible, secretly, in order to keep the king quite unprepared. This is how he collected them. He sent word to the governors of all the garrisons he had in various cities, to enlist as many Peloponnesians as they could find, and the best, pretending that Tissaphernes was plotting against the cities. For in fact the Ionian colonies had belonged to Tissaphernes originally, being given him by the king; but then they had gone over to Cyros, all except Miletos. In Miletos, however, Tissaphernes had got wind beforehand that the people were going to do the same, and revolt to Cyros, and he had killed some and banished others. Cyros gave refuge to the banished men, and collected an army, and laid siege to Miletos by land and sea, and tried to restore the banished: this was another excuse for him to assemble his army. He sent also to the king, and asked him as his brother to give him those cities rather than let Tissaphernes rule over them; and his mother worked to help him. Thus the king did not see the plot against himself, but he thought that war with Tissaphernes was why he spent so much money on the army. He did not worry about fighting between Cyros and Tissaphernes, especially as Cyros was careful to send in the proper tribute from the cities that Tissaphernes had in his province.

Another army was being collected for him in the Chersonese, opposite Abydos, in the following manner. Clearchos was a Lacedaimonian exile; Cyros met him, and admired him, and gave him 10,000 darics.[1] Using this money to collect a force, he made war, with the Chersonese as his base, upon the Thracians who are settled farther up above the Hellespont, and since he thus helped the Hellenes, the Hellenic cities willingly contributed to the support of

[1] a Persian gold coin weighing about 128 grains

his men. In such way this army again was being secretly kept for Cyros. Besides, Aristippos the Thessalian was his friend; and he being hard pressed by the opposing party at home, came to Cyros and asked him to provide three months' pay for 2,000 men, which he thought would be enough to get the better of his rivals. Cyros gave him six months' pay for 4,000, and requested him not to make friends with his rivals without consulting him. There again was an army in Thessaly being kept ready unnoticed. Proxenos the Bœotian was another friend; Cyros begged him to get as many men as he could and join him, since he was about to attack the Pisidians who were making themselves a nuisance to his country. Two other friends, Sophainetos the Stymphalian and Socrates the Achaian, he told to join him with as large forces as possible, because he was going to make war on Tissaphernes along with the Milesian exiles. And so they did.

II

When he thought the time had come to march up country he made the excuse that he wanted to expel the Pisidians from the land altogether; and he summoned both his national forces and the Hellenic to meet for this purpose. He also sent word to Clearchos to bring up all his army; and to Aristippos, to make terms with his rivals at home and to send the whole army to himself. He ordered Xenias also, who was in general command of the foreign troops in the cities, to bring them all up except as many as were enough to garrison the fortresses, and except those who were besieging Miletos; the exiles he told to come too, promising them that if he should succeed in his purpose, he would not cease until he could restore them to their home. They obeyed gladly, for they trusted him, and proceeded to Sardis under arms.

Accordingly Xenias came also to Sardis with about 4,000

men-at-arms; Proxenos was there with 1,500 and 500 light-armed men, Sophainetos the Stymphalian with 1,000 men-at-arms, Socrates the Achaian with about 500, Pasion the Megarian with 300 men-at-arms and 300 targeteers; he and Socrates had been among those besieging Miletos. This was the force that assembled at Sardis; Tissaphernes took note of this, and thought it was too large for the Pisidians, and so he marched to the king as quickly as possible with 500 horse. And the king made preparations to resist Cyros's plan, when he heard about it from Tissaphernes.

Cyros then, with the forces I have mentioned, set out from Sardis. Three stages, 22 leagues,[1] brought him as far as the River Maiandros. The river is 200 feet wide, with a bridge supported on floating vessels. Crossing this, he travelled through Phrygia, one stage, 8 leagues, to Colossai, an inhabited city, large and prosperous. There he stayed seven days; and there Menon the Thessalian joined him, with 1,000 men-at-arms and 500 targeteers, Dolopians and Ainanians and Olynthians. Thence he passed on three stages, 20 leagues, to Celainai, an inhabited city of Phrygia, large and prosperous.

There Cyros had a palace, and a great park full of wild animals, which he used to hunt on horseback when he wished to exercise himself and his horses. Through this park flows the River Maiandros, and the source is in the palace; it flows also through the city of Celainai. There is also a palace of the Great King in Celainai, deserted, at the source of the River Marsyas under the Acropolis; this river also flows through the city and discharges into the Maiandros: the width of the Marsyas is 25 feet. There it is said Apollo flayed Marsyas,[2] who had challenged him to a music-match, and hung up the skin in the cave where the source is; and therefore the river is named Marsyas. This palace and the fortress Xerxes is said to have built when he came back after the defeat in Greece. There Cyros

[1] The parasang was a little over three miles. The plethron is about 101 feet: I call it 100. The men-at-arms are hoplites in heavy armour, the targeteers peltasts with light shields, light troops.

[2] Marsyas the satyr picked up Athena's hoboy, which she threw away because it made her look ugly to blow it; and he was so pleased with himself that he challenged Apollo to a match.

remained thirty days; and Clearchos the Lacedaimonian exile joined him, with 1,000 men-at-arms, and 800 Thracian targeteers, and 200 Cretan bowmen. At the same time Sosis the Syracusan came in with 300 men-at-arms, and Sophainetos with 1,000 from Arcadia. There Cyros held a review, and counted the Hellenic mercenaries in the park; there were in all 11,000 men-at-arms, and about 2,000 targeteers.

III

From this place he marched two stages, 10 leagues, to Peltai, an inhabited city, where he stayed three days. In this halt Xenias the Arcadian celebrated the feast Lycaia and held sports; the prizes were golden skin-scrapers,[1] and Cyros looked on at the contest. From there he marched two stages, 12 leagues, to Potters' Market, an inhabited city, on the boundary of Mysia. From there he marched three stages, 30 leagues, to the plain of the Caystros, an inhabited city, where he stayed five days. More than three months' wages were now due to the soldiers, and they came often to his door to ask for it. He talked of expectations and put them off; but he was clearly annoyed, for it was not the way of Cyros, if he had, not to give. At this place came to Cyros Epyaxa, wife of Syennesis, King of the Cilicians, and she was said to have given him large sums of money, so Cyros paid the army four months' wages. The Cilician queen had a bodyguard of Cilicians and Aspendians; and Cyros was said to have been intimate with her.

Thence he marched two stages, 10 leagues, to Thymbrion, an inhabited city. There by the side of the road was the spring named after Midas the Phrygian king, where Midas was said to have caught the Satyr by mixing wine with the water. Thence two stages, 10 leagues, to Tyriaion, an inhabited city, where he stayed three days. The Cilician is

---

[1] used in the bath, and usually made of iron

said to have begged him to show her a display of the army. So he reviewed his troops, national and Hellenic, on the plain.

He ordered the Hellenes to put themselves in battle array after their own fashion, each captain commanding his own men. So they paraded four deep; Menon held the right wing and Clearchos the left, the others in the centre. First Cyros inspected the nationals; they marched past in troops of horse and companies of foot. Then the Hellenes, Cyros driving by in a car and the Cilician in her state wagon. All the men wore bronze helmets and purple tunics and greaves, and had their shields uncovered. When he had driven by them all he halted his car in front of the central line, and sent Pigres the interpreter to the Hellenic captains, with the order to present pikes and advance the whole line. The captains passed on the order to the men; and when the trumpet sounded they presented pikes and advanced. Then the pace quickened. The men doubled towards the tents with cheers of their own accord. There was a panic among the national troops, and the Cilician fled in her wagon, and the people from the market fled too, leaving their goods behind. The Cilician was amazed to see the brilliancy and discipline of the army; and Cyros was delighted when he saw how the natives were scared by the Hellenes.

From this place he went three stages, 20 leagues, to Iconion, the last city of Phrygia, where he stayed three days. Thence he marched through Lycaonia five stages, 30 leagues. He gave this part over to the Hellenes to despoil as enemy country. After that Cyros sent the Cilician back to her own country the quickest way, and with her he sent Menon and his men. But Cyros marched along with the others through Cappadocia four stages, 25 leagues, to Dana, an inhabited city, large and prosperous, where they stayed three days. Here Cyros put to death a Persian,

Megaphernes, one who wore the royal purple,[1] and another high official, one of the lieutenant-governors, on the charge of conspiracy against him.

After that they tried to break into Cilicia; but the entry was a carriage road, very straight and impossible for an army to enter if anyone resisted. Syennesis was said to be on the heights guarding the pass, and Cyros therefore stayed one day in the plain. But next day news came that Syennesis had left the heights when he found that Menon's force already was in Cilicia and behind the mountains, and that a fleet of war under Tamôs was sailing round to Cilicia from Ionia, a fleet that belonged to the Lacedaimonians and to Cyros himself. So Cyros came up that pass into the mountains without opposition, and saw the tents where the Cilicians had been on the watch.

After that he came down into a large and beautiful plain, well watered, and full of all sorts of trees and vines, bearing plenty of sesamum, too, and millet and barley and wheat; a strong and lofty wall of mountains surrounds it everywhere from sea to sea. Coming down he marched through this plain four stages, 25 leagues, to Tarsus, a city of Cilicia both large and prosperous, where was the palace of Syennesis, King of Cilicia; through the midst of the city flows a river called Cydnos, 200 feet across. The inhabitants, with Syennesis, had left it and gone to a strong place in the hills, except those who had goods for sale; those who lived by the sea also remained, and those in Soli and Issos. Epyaxa, the wife of Syennesis, had reached Tarsus five days before Cyros; but in crossing the mountains two companies of Menon's force had been lost; some said they had been cut down by the Cilicians while plundering, others that they had been left behind and could not find their party, and lost their way and wandered about till they perished. In any case they were a hundred men-at-arms. When the others came in they were enraged at the destruc-

[1] the highest rank, others wearing purple facings only

tion of their comrades, and plundered Tarsus and the palace there. When Cyros entered the place he summoned Syennesis; but Syennesis said he had never yet put himself in the hands of one stronger than himself, and he would not come to Cyros then, until his wife persuaded him and got promises of safety. After this, when they met, Syennesis gave Cyros large sums of money for his campaign, and Cyros gave him such gifts as are thought honourable for a king, a horse with golden bit and bridle, and a gold necklace and bracelets, and a gold scimitar and Persian robes, and promised no more to plunder the country; he should have back the captives whenever he found any.

There Cyros and the army stayed twenty days, for the soldiers said they would go no farther; they already suspected that they were marching against the king, and said they had not been hired for that. Clearchos first tried to compel his men to go on; but they pelted him and his animals as soon as started, and Clearchos had a narrow escape then of being stoned to death, but after he saw he could not compel them he called a public meeting of all the men. He began by standing before them for some time with tears running down his cheeks, and the men were silent in surprise; then he spoke as follows:

"Men and comrades, don't be surprised that I am deeply hurt by what has happened. Cyros has been my friend; when I was banished from my country, he treated me with respect, and also gave me ten thousand darics; and when I received this money I did not put it by as my own, or spend it on luxuries, but I spent it on you. Then first I made war on the Thracians, and with your help punished them for the wrongs of Hellas. I drove them from the Chersonese, where they wished to rob our countrymen of their land. Afterwards, when Cyros called me, I marched with you to him, that if he needed me I might show my gratitude for his benefits. But since you will not march with me, I must of necessity either desert you and enjoy his friendship, or else deceive him and stay with you. If it will be right I do not know; but in any case I will choose you, and with you suffer whatever I must suffer. No-one shall ever say that I led Hellenes against savages, and then deserted the Hellenes and chose the friendship of savages; but since you will not obey me, I will go with you and suffer whatever I must suffer. For I consider that you are my country and my friends and comrades; and with you, I think I shall be honoured wherever I may be, but without you, I think I am not able either to help a friend or hurt an enemy. Where you go there I will go also: that is my resolve."

So he spoke, and the soldiers all cheered him, both his own and the others who heard, when he said he would not march against the king; and more than two thousand from Xenias and Pasion took their arms and baggage and encamped beside Clearchos.

Cyros was very much upset and did not know what to do. He sent for Clearchos, but Clearchos did not wish to go himself; he sent him a message, however, unknown to the soldiers, and told him not to worry, all would turn out well; but he should go on sending for him, and he would refuse to come. After that he collected his own men, and those who had joined him, and anyone else who liked, and spoke to them after this fashion:

"Men and comrades, it is clear now how things are between us and Cyros: we are no longer his men, since we do not follow him; and he no longer finds our pay. He thinks you are in the wrong, I know; and that is why I will not go when he sends for me. The chief reason is, I am ashamed, because my conscience tells me I have broken faith with him altogether; next I am afraid that if he catches me he may punish me for the wrong he thinks I have done. Then I think it is no time for us to sleep or neglect ourselves; we

must make some plan. As long as we remain here I think
we must arrange to be as safe as possible; or if we decide
to go at once, we must arrange to go as safely as possible
and to find provisions, for without this there's no good in a
captain and no good in a man. But this man is worth much
as a friend, and very dangerous as an enemy: he has forces
in foot and horse and fleet, which we all see and understand quite well. Indeed, I don't think we should sit here
any longer. So now's the time to say what is best; speak up,
someone."

He said this and ceased; and people got up, some of
themselves to tell what they proposed, others prompted by
him, who pointed out what a mess they were in without
the support of Cyros, whether they stayed or marched. One
indeed pretended he was in a hurry that they should march
for Hellas as quickly as they could, and told them to choose
captains with all expedition, if Clearchos did not want to
lead them; provisions they must buy (there was a market
in the national army) and pack up their traps; they must
go and ask Cyros for ships to sail in; if he would not grant
this, ask him for a guide to see they travelled among friends.
If he would not give so much as a guide, they must put
themselves in order at once and send men on ahead to occupy the heights, or else Cyros might get there first, or the
Cilicians—don't forget we have taken many of them and
their goods. After this speech Clearchos got up and said:

"Me to be captain of this march—let no-one say such a
thing! I see many reasons why I cannot do that. But I
will be ruled by the man you choose, whoever he may be,
to show you I know how to obey as well as any man on
earth!"

After this another got up, and showed how silly the man
was who advised them to ask Cyros for ships. Did they
think he would turn his fleet backwards? How silly to ask

for a guide from a man when we have just spoilt his business! And if we trust the guide he gives us, what hinders
him from giving orders to occupy the heights first? "I
should be sorry myself to embark in any ships he might
give. Suppose he sinks us and the ships! I should be afraid
to follow the guide he might give. Suppose he leads us to a
place we can't get out from! I should wish to get away
without his consent, unnoticed; and that is impossible. I tell
you all this is nonsense. I propose that Clearchos go with
suitable people, and ask what Cyros means to do with us;
and if his business now is like what he did with other
hired soldiers before, that we follow him too and show ourselves no worse than those whom he brought up country
earlier; but if the business is bigger than the other, and
more difficult and dangerous, demand that he either persuade us and we will go, or be persuaded and let us depart
in friendship. In that way, if we follow him we shall be
friends and follow willingly, and if we depart we shall depart safely. Let them report to us whatever he says; he will
listen and decide accordingly."

This was agreed; they chose the persons and sent them
with Clearchos, and they asked Cyros the questions which
the army thought proper. He answered, that he heard an
enemy of his, Abrocomas, was on the River Euphrates
twelve stages away; he said he wanted to march against
this man, and if he was there he wished to punish him, but
if he were gone, we will consider what to do. The chosen
men reported this answer to the soldiers; they had a suspicion that he was leading them against the king, still all
the same they decided to follow. But they asked more pay;
and Cyros promised to pay them all half as much again
as they had had before, instead of one daric, one and a half
each month per man; but as to the king, no-one heard one
single word about that, in public at least.

IV

From that place he marched two stages, 10 leagues, to the River Pharos, which was 300 feet across. Thence one stage, 5 leagues, to the River Pyramos, 1 furlong wide. Thence two stages, 15 leagues, to Issoi, the last inhabited city of Cilicia, lying by the seaside, a large and prosperous place, where they stayed three days. There the ships from the Peloponnese joined Cyros, thirty-five with a Lacedaimonian admiral, Pythagoras. Tamôs the Egyptian piloted them from Ephesos, and he brought five and twenty other ships belonging to Cyros, with which he had besieged Miletos while it was friendly to Tissaphernes and fought against him for Cyros. A Lacedaimonian Cheirisophos was also in this fleet, sent for by Cyros; and he brought 700 men-at-arms, whose captain was on the side of Cyros. The ships were anchored opposite Cyros's tent. There were also the Hellenic mercenaries from Abrocomas, 400 men-at-arms; they had left him and come over to Cyros for his expedition against the king.

From that place he marched one stage, 5 leagues, to the Gates of Cilicia and Syria. These were two forts; the inner one, in front of Cilicia, was held by Syennesis and a Cilician garrison; the other one, in front of Syria, was said to be held by a king's garrison. Between the two forts runs a river named Carsos, 100 feet wide. The whole distance between the two forts was 3 furlongs. No force could get through; for the pass was narrow, and the walls ran down to the sea, and above were high-clambering rocks: both fortresses had gates. Because of this pass Cyros had sent for the ships; he would land forces both within and without the gates, and fight his way through the enemy if they were protecting the Syrian Gates, which he expected Abrocomas to do with a large army. But Abrocomas did not do this: when he heard Cyros was in Cilicia, he left Phoenicia and marched to the king, with an army of 300,000 as it was reported.

From here Cyros marched through Syria one stage, 5 leagues, to Myriandros, a city inhabited by Phoenicians beside the sea: the place was a port of trade, and a great many merchant ships were anchored there. In this place he stayed seven days. Here Xenias the Arcadian and Pasion the Megarian put their valuables aboard a ship and sailed off; being offended, as most people thought, because Cyros allowed Clearchos to keep the men who had deserted to Clearchos, when they meant to go back to Hellas and not against the king. When these two could not be found, word went about that Cyros was in pursuit with warships; some hoped the cowards would be caught, others pitied them if they should be caught. But Cyros called a meeting of the captains and said:

"Xenias and Pasion have left us. But be sure they have not deserted: I know where they have gone. Nor have they escaped: I have galleys to catch their boat. But by God I will not pursue them! No-one shall say that I use a man while he is with me, but if he wants to go I catch him and maltreat him and rob him of his goods. Let them go, and remember that they treat us worse than we treat them. Indeed I have their wives and children still, guarded in Tralles; but they shall not lose them. They shall have them again in return for their good service so far."

That was what he said. And when the Hellenes heard the fine spirit of Cyros, if anyone was rather discouraged about the enterprise, they went on more happily and more willingly.

After this, Cyros marched four stages, 20 leagues, to the River Chalos, 100 feet wide, which was full of large tame fish, which the Syrians, revering as gods, would not let anyone hurt—or the pigeons either. The villages where they encamped belonged to Parysatis, given for the queen's girdle.[1] Thence he marched five stages, 30 leagues, to the source of the River Dardas, breadth 100 feet. There was the

[1] like others, given her for such excuses as perquisites

palace of Belesys, the ruler of Syria, and a park large and beautiful, which contains all the kindly fruits of the earth. But Cyros cut down the trees and burnt the palace. From there, three stages, 15 leagues, to the Euphrates, half a mile in width; and a large prosperous town was there named Thapsacos, where he stayed five days.

Then Cyros assembled the Hellenic captains, and told them their road was to the Great King at Babylon; they were to inform the men and persuade them to follow. So they called a public meeting and informed them. The men were angry with their captains, and said they had known this all along and hidden it from them; said they would not march, unless they were paid as the former expedition had been which had marched up country with Cyros to the father of Cyros, and then not for battle but invited by the father of Cyros. This the captains reported to Cyros; and he promised to give each man five minas of silver when they reached Babylon, and pay in full until he should bring the Hellenes back to Ionia.

Most of them agreed to this offer. But Menon mustered his own detachment apart, before it was clear what the other captains would do, and said to them:

"Men, listen to me. You will be able to win credit with Cyros above the others, without danger and without trouble. Then what do I advise you to do? Now Cyros asks the Hellenes to follow him against the king: I say you ought to cross the Euphrates before it is clear what the others will answer. If they vote to follow, you will be thought to be the cause, by crossing first; Cyros will think you the most ready and willing, and he will thank you and prove his gratitude—he knows how to do that better than anyone. If they vote against, we shall all go back together, but you he will trust most as the only ones ready to obey, and he will put you in charge of garrisons or other commands;

whatever else you may want, I know you will find Cyros
a friend."

When they heard this, they complied, and went across
before the others made any answer. Cyros was delighted
when he heard they had crossed, and sent Glûs to tell them
so: he said:

"I am pleased with you now, men, and I will take care
you shall be pleased with me, or my name is no longer
Cyros!"

The soldiers were in high hopes, and prayed good fortune
for him; it was said also that he sent magnificent gifts for
Menon.[1] Then Cyros crossed, and the whole army followed.
In the crossing, no-one was wetted above the breast. The
people of Thapsacos said that this river had never been
fordable for foot soldiers before that; it could be crossed
only by boats, and Abrocomas had burnt them all on his
way past, that Cyros might not cross. This was believed
to be a sign from heaven, and the river had plainly made
way for Cyros as destined to be king.

From that place he marched through Syria nine stages,
50 leagues, as far as the River Araxes. Many villages were
there, full of corn and wine; there they stayed three days
and got provisions.

v

Thence he marched through Arabia, keeping the Euphrates on the right, five stages of desert, 35 leagues. In
this part the country was one great flat plain like a sea, but
covered with absinth; whatever there was besides of wood
or reeds, all were sweet-smelling like spices. There was
no tree, but all sorts of animals, troops of wild asses, plenty
of ostriches, bustards also and gazelles; and the horsemen
often chased these. The asses, if they were chased, ran ahead
and stood still, for they ran much faster than horses; again

[1] Menon figures in Plato as fond of money, and "the spoilt child of
fortune."

when the horses came near they ran as before, and they could not be caught unless the horsemen placed themselves at intervals and hunted in relays. The meat of those caught was like venison but more tender. No-one caught an ostrich; horsemen in chase soon gave up, for she got far away before them, running on her feet and flying too, using her wings like a sail. Bustards, however, can be caught if you put them up smartly, for they fly in short spurts like a partridge and quickly tire. Their flesh was very good.

Marching through this country they came to the River Mascas, width 100 feet. There was a great deserted city named Corsote; this was surrounded by the Mascas, and there they stayed three days and got provisions. From that place he marched thirteen desert stages, 90 leagues, keeping the Euphrates on his right, until he reached the Gates. In these stages many of the baggage-animals were starved to death, for there was neither grass nor any sort of tree, but the whole country was bare: the natives used to dig up grinding-stones beside the river and shape them, and these they took to Babylon and sold them there, and bought corn to feed themselves. Corn failed the army, and none could be bought except in the Lydian market which Cyros had in his national camp, four shekels for a capith of wheat or barley: the shekel is worth seven and a half Attic obols, and the capith is two Attic quarts.[1] So the men had to manage by eating meat. Some of the stages were very long, when he wished to get on to water or grass.

Once indeed when there was a narrow way and deep mud, bad going for the carriages, Cyros took charge with the noblest and richest of his staff, and ordered Glûs and Pigres to take some of his nationals and get the carriages through. As they seemed to be lazy about it, he was angry, and told the noble Persians beside him to lend a hand with the wagons. Then could be seen something of his discipline. Each man of them threw off his purple robe where he stood,

---

[1] The Attic drachma contained six obols; so $7\frac{1}{2}$ is $1\frac{1}{4}$ drachmas. The quart, or choinix, was a man's daily allowance of corn, minimum.

and away they went as one might run a race! Down the steep hill they went, in their costly tunics and embroidered breeches, and some with necklaces round their necks and bracelets on their arms; in this garb they jumped straight into the mud, and quicker than one could think possible they got the wagons clear.

Take it in all, Cyros showed himself to be in earnest throughout the march, and wasted no time except where he had to sit still for vittling or some other necessity. For he thought that the quicker he came, the less prepared for the fight would the king be. And it was easy to see for any sensible man that the king's empire might be strong in extent and population, but it was weak by the long distances between his scattered forces if war were made suddenly with speed.

On the other side of the Euphrates in the desert was a city great and prosperous named Charmande; from this place the soldiers bought provisions, and they crossed on rafts in this way. They took the skins which they used to cover their tents and stuffed them with hay, then folded and sewed them up to keep the water from the hay. On these they crossed, and got their provisions, wine made from dates and millet corn, which was commonest in that country.

There was some quarrel there between Menon's soldiers and those of Clearchos, when Clearchos judged that one of Menon's men was in the wrong and flogged him. Menon went and told his party; the men were displeased and very angry with Clearchos. On the same day Clearchos had gone to the crossing place, and after inspecting the market there he rode back to his tent with a few followers through Menon's camp. Cyros had not yet come, but he was on the way. One of Menon's men splitting wood saw Clearchos riding past, and threw the axe at him. This man missed him, but another threw a stone, and another, then many with shouts and cries. Clearchos got away into his own camp, and at once called them to arms; he told his own men to lean their shields against their knees,[1] and himself with the Thracians and horsemen he had in the camp, more than forty but mostly Thracians, he rode for Menon's division. These were astounded and so was Menon, and all ran for their arms, some standing still on the spot in dismay. Proxenos happened to come in behind them with a company of his men-at-arms, and he went straight in between them and grounded arms, and begged Clearchos to desist. But Clearchos was angry to hear his danger lightly spoken of when he had hardly escaped being stoned to death, and told him to get out of the way.

At this moment Cyros came up and asked what the matter was. At once he took his javelin in hand and galloped in with those of his bodyguard that he had with him and said:

"Now then, Clearchos and Proxenos and you others, you don't know what you are doing. If you make a fight among yourselves, understand that you will cut me to pieces this very day, and yourselves very soon after me! For if anything goes wrong with us, these people you see round us here will all be worse enemies to us than the king's army."

Clearchos came to himself when he heard this; both parties desisted, and went back quietly to their own quarters.

VI

As they moved onwards from this place tracks of horses appeared, and dung; there seemed to be traces of something like two thousand horses. They were going in front and burning the grass and anything else that was useful. Orontas, a Persian who was there, himself one of the royal family, and said to be one of the best men in Persia in military matters, made a treacherous proposal. He had form-

---

[1] ready to receive cavalry

erly been at war with Cyros but made it up; now he told
Cyros that if he would give him a thousand horsemen, he
would either lie in wait for this incinerating vanguard and
kill the lot, or else bring in a good many and stop their incinerating, and he would take care that they should never
be able to see Cyros's army and take the news to the king.
Cyros thought this sounded like useful advice, and he told
him to take a part from each of the commanders. So
Orontas thought the horsemen were there ready for him,
and wrote a letter to the king that he would come and
bring with him as many horsemen as possible; he must
warn his own cavalry to receive him as a friend. In the
letter were also reminders of their former friendship and
trust. This letter he gave to a trusty man, as he thought;
but the man took it and gave it to Cyros. Cyros read it,
and arrested Orontas, and summoned to his own tent seven
of the noblest men about him, and directed the Hellenic
captains to bring armed men and post them around his
tent. They did so, and brought some three thousand men-
at-arms. He invited Clearchos in to be one of the court,
for he thought him to be the leading man among all the
Hellenes, and this was the public opinion too. Afterwards
he told his friends how Cyros conducted the courtmartial;
for it was no secret.

Cyros began in this way: "I have summoned you, my
friends, that I may consult you what is right to do before
God and man, and so I may do about Orontas, who is here.
This man was first given me by my father to be my subject.
Then under orders, as he said himself, from my brother,
he made war against me when he held the fortress of Sardis;
and I took up the challenge and made him decide to cease
war against me, and we clasped hands, and after that, is
there any wrong I have done you, Orontas?" He said "No."
Again Cyros asked. "Then I did you no wrong after that,
as you admit yourself, but did you desert to the Mysians

and damage my country as much as you could?" Orontas said "Yes." "Very well," said Cyros; "when you found out your own weakness, did you take refuge at the altar of Artemis, and say you were sorry, and did I believe you, and did we both pledge loyalty and friendship together?" This also Orontas acknowledged. "Then what wrong have I done you now," said Cyros, "that for the third time you have been discovered planning treachery against me?" Orontas said that he had suffered no wrong, and Cyros asked: "Do you admit, then, that you have done wrong to me?" "I can't help it," said Orontas. Then Cyros asked again: "And could you ever become an enemy to my brother again, and a faithful friend to me?" He answered, "Even if I should, Cyros, you would never believe it." Then Cyros turned to the court and said, "That is what the man has done, you hear what he says. You speak first, Clearchos; what is your judgment?" Clearchos said, "My advice is to get rid of this man at once, that we need not be obliged to watch him, but we may have leisure from him to do our best for these willing helpers." He said the others agreed with this judgment. After this, he said, at the bidding of Cyros, all those present, including the man's kinsmen, rose and took hold of the girdle of Orontas as a sign that he must die; then he was led away by those whose duty it was. But those who did reverence to him before, did reverence then, when they saw him, although they knew he was being led away to death.

He was taken into the tent of Artapates, the most trusty of all Cyros's wandbearers, but after that no-one ever saw Orontas alive or dead, and no-one who knew ever told how he died. People guessed all sorts of things, but no tomb of Orontas was ever seen.

VII

From that place he marched through Babylonia three stages, 12 leagues. In the third stage Cyros held a review of Hellenes and national troops on the plain at midnight, for he thought the king would be there at the coming dawn with his army, to fight. He ordered Clearchos to lead the right wing, and Menon the Thessalian the left, and he arranged his own troops himself. After the review, with the daylight deserters came in from the Great King, and reported to Cyros about the king's army.

Cyros invited the captains and other officers of the Hellenes, and held council how he should arrange the battle, and offered this cheering advice. "Gentlemen," he said, "not for want of men have I brought you here as my allies, but I believe you to be better and stronger than large numbers of my own countrymen, and that is why I did it. Show yourselves men, therefore, worthy of the freedom which you possess and which I envy. Be sure I would give all I have and many times over if I could get that freedom. But I understand what a contest you have before you, and I will tell you, that you may understand also. The numbers are enormous, and they will come on with loud shouts and cries; but if you can stand that, I am ashamed to think what kind of men you will find in this country. If you show yourselves men, and if all goes well with my part, I will arrange that any one of you who wishes to return home will be the envy of those he meets at home; but I think I shall persuade many of you to choose what I have here rather than what he will find at home."

Then Gaulites, a Samian exile who was present, and a true friend of Cyros, said, "Oh yes, Cyros, but some do say that you can promise great things now, because all this danger is threatening, but you will not remember if all goes well, so they say; some say that even if you do remember, with the best of will you cannot pay all you promise." Cyros listened, and said, "Well, gentlemen, my father's empire reaches southwards as far as where it is too hot for men to live, and northwards to where it is too cold; all between is under the governance of my brother's friends.

If we are victorious, I must make my friends masters of all this. So I have no fear that I may not have something to give to each of my friends; what I fear is that there may not be friends enough. And to each of you Hellenes I will give a golden crown."

On hearing this they were much more cheerful and eager themselves, and they reported it to the others. Besides the Hellenic captains, many others paid Cyros a visit, asking what they would get if they won, and he sent them all away satisfied.

All that spoke with him begged him not to expose himself in the battle, but to take post behind themselves. At this crisis Clearchos asked him once, "Do you really think he'll fight with you, Cyros, your own brother?" "I'm sure he will," said Cyros, "if he is really the son of Dareios and Parysatis, if he really is my brother—not without a battle shall I win this prize."

At the review the numbers were: Hellenes, shields 10,400, targeteers 2,500; national troops with Cyros, 100,000, and scythe-bearing chariots about 20. The enemy were said to be 1,200,000, with 200 scythe-bearing chariots. There were 6,000 cavalry besides, under Artagerses; these again were posted before the king himself. The royal army was commanded by four marshals or generals, each having 300,000 men under him—Abrocomas, Tissaphernes, Gobryas, Arbaces. But of these not all were present in the battle, only 900,000 men and 150 scythe-bearing chariots; for Abrocomas came five days too late, having to march from Phoenicia. This was what the deserter reported to Cyros before the battle, and after the battle those that were left of the enemy said the same.

From this place Cyros marched one stage, 3 leagues, with the whole army in array both national and Hellenic, for he thought the king would fight on that day. Half-way through that stage a deep trench had been dug, five fathoms

across, three fathoms deep. The trench extended inland
for twelve leagues over the plain as far as the wall of Media.
(Here are the canals bringing water from the River Tigris;
there are four, 100 feet wide and very deep, and barges of
corn ply upon them; they discharge into the Euphrates,
and are one league apart, with bridges over them.) Along
the Euphrates was a narrow path, 20 feet in width, between
the river and the end of the trench. This trench the Great
King had made for a defence when he learnt that Cyros
was coming. Cyros and his army now passed along this
path, and so they came inside the trench.

So on this day the king did not fight, but there were many
tracks of men and horses retreating. Here Cyros called
Silanos the Ambraciot seer, and paid him 3,000 darics for
his bet, because eleven days before he had declared at the
sacrifice that the king would not fight within ten days,
and Cyros said, "Then he won't fight at all, if he does not
fight within ten days; and if your words come true, I promise you ten talents." So he paid him the money then, because
ten days were past. But since here at the trench the king did
not try to hinder the passage of Cyros and his army, both
Cyros and the others believed he had given up the thought
of fighting; so the next day Cyros marched more carelessly,
and the day after he was leading the way seated in his
chariot, with a small body of men in front, while most
of the army was in disorder and the soldiers had left much
of their heavy arms to be carried by wagons or pack animals.

It was already about full-market time,[1] and the stage
where they were to rest was near, when Pategyas, a trusty
Persian from the staff of Cyros, suddenly appeared galloping
on a sweating horse, and shouted out straight to all he met,
in Greek and Persian, that the king with a large army was
coming prepared for battle. Then there was great confusion.
The Hellenes thought, and so did all, that they would be
attacked on the spot in this disorder; and Cyros leapt from

[1] 9 or 10 a.m.

his car and put on his corselet and got on his horse and took his lances in hand, and sent word to all the rest to arm and take post every man.

At once they fell in with all haste, Clearchos holding the right wing on the Euphrates River, Proxenos next, and then the others, with Menon commanding the left wing of the Hellenic forces. Of the national troops, 1,000 Paphlagonian horsemen took stand by Clearchos on the right, and the Hellenic targeteers; in the left wing, Ariaios, Cyros's second-in-command, and the other nationals; and Cyros with his 600 cavalry in the centre, all except Cyros being armed with corselets and thigh pieces and helmets, but Cyros went into battle with bare head—it is said that the Persians generally risk fighting with the head bare. All the horses wore protections on forehead and breast, and the horsemen had Hellenic swords.

It was already midday, and the enemy had not appeared; but when afternoon came dust appeared like a white cloud, and some time afterwards a sort of blackness spreading far over the plain. But when they came nearer, quickly there were flashes of bronze and spears and the lines were visible. Cavalry in white corselets were on the enemy's left wing; Tissaphernes was said to be in command of these. Next came wickershieldmen, next men-at-arms with wooden shields which reached to their feet—these were said to be Egyptians; then more cavalry, bowmen too. All these were arranged by nations, each nation marching as a solid square of men. In front of all were the chariots, with large spaces between, those which are called scythe-bearers. They had the scythes sticking out sideways from the axle-trees and under the cars pointing downwards, to cut through any they met. The notion was to drive at the companies of Hellenes and cut them through.

When Cyros had warned them not to mind the shouts and cries of the barbarians, he made a mistake; there was

no shouting, but they came on in deep silence quietly in
step, and slowly.

At this moment, Cyros, riding past with Pigres the interpreter and three or four others, shouted out to Clearchos
to lead his lines against the enemy centre, because the king
was there: "If we beat that," he said, "we have won!"
Clearchos eyed the mass in the middle, and learnt from Cyros that the king was outside in the Hellenic left (for the
king so much exceeded in numbers that with his centre he
overlapped Cyros's left); he still was unwilling to break
away the right wing from the river for fear he might be
turned on both flanks, so he answered Cyros that he would
take care that all went well.

At this crisis the Persian army was advancing evenly, but
the Hellenic line was halted as the men kept coming up
and forming. Cyros was riding some way off from his
army, and looking keenly at each side, staring at the enemy
and his own men. An Athenian, Xenophon, saw him and
went out to him from the Hellenic line, and asked if he
had any orders. Cyros drew rein, and told him to spread
the news everywhere that the omens from the sacrifice were
all favourable. As he was speaking, he heard a confused
noise running through the ranks, and asked what the noise
was. The other said that the word of the day was being
passed round for the second time. Cyros wondered who
gave the word, and what it was. He answered: "Zeus Saviour and Victory." Cyros said, "I accept the omen, so be
it!" As he spoke he rode away to his own place.

The two lines were hardly six or seven hundred yards
apart when the Hellenes began to chant the battle hymn
and moved against the enemy. Part of the line billowed out
as they moved, and the slower part began to double up;
then all together broke into a ringing cheer, "Eleleu, eleleu!" and all charged at the double. Some say they also
beat the spears on the shields to scare the horses. Before one

shot reached them, the barbarians turned and fled. At once the Hellenes pursued with might and main, but shouted to each other, "Don't run races! Keep your line!" The chariots ran away without drivers, some through their own people, some through the Hellenes: these saw them coming, and gave them room. One man was caught as he stood like someone dazed in the middle of a racecourse; even this fellow had no hurt, so they said, and not one other Hellene was hurt in this battle, except one on the left wing, said to have been shot by an arrow.

Cyros was delighted when he saw the Hellenes victorious in their part and pursuing; he was greeted as king already by those about him, but even so he was not induced to join the pursuit. He kept his own body of 600 horse in close order, and watched to see what the king would do. He knew of course that the king held the centre of the Persian army. Indeed all the generals of these barbarian nations hold the centre when they command; they consider it to be safest when their force is on both sides, and if they need to send dispatches, the army knows in half the time. So the king was then holding the centre of his army, and still overlapping the left wing of Cyros. Since there was no enemy in front, and none against the troops drawn up before him, he wheeled round to encircle Cyros. Then Cyros, fearing he might get behind and cut up the Hellenic force, charged at him; with his 600 he fell on the troops posted in front of the king, and put the 6,000 men to flight, and it is said killed with his own hand their commander Artagerses. When those were routed, Cyros's 600 were broken up in the pursuit, except a very few left about him, hardly more than his table-companions, as they were called.

Left with these, he caught sight of the king and the bodyguard round him; then he could hold himself no longer, but charged at him, saying, "I see the man!" and struck him on the breast and wounded him through his corselet, as the doctor Ctesias reports, who says he cured the wound. As he struck, someone struck Cyros with a lance violently under the eye; and there as they fought, the king and Cyros and the others about each, how many fell of the king's party Ctesias tells, for he was in attendance; and Cyros himself was killed, and eight of the most noble about him lay dead over his body. It is said that Artapates, who was the most trusted of all his wandholders, when he saw Cyros fallen leaped off his horse and threw himself on the body. Some say the king told a man to cut his throat over the body, some that he killed himself with his own scimitar—he had a golden scimitar, and he wore bracelets and armlets and the other ornaments of the noblest Persians; for he was highly honoured by Cyros for loyalty and trustworthiness.

VIII

So died Cyros; of all Persians that came after the first Cyros, the most royal and most worthy to be king, as all agree who are reputed to have known Cyros themselves. To begin with, when he was still a boy, and being educated along with his brother and the other boys, he was considered best of them all in everything. For all the sons of the noblest Persians are educated at the king's door; there one may learn many a lesson in good manners, but nothing ugly can be heard or seen there. They see and hear when honour is done to any by the king, and when others are disgraced; so from boyhood they learn both to rule and to be ruled. There Cyros was thought to be the most modest of all his agemates, obeying his elders better than his own inferiors did.

Next, he was the greatest lover of horses, and knew best how to manage them; and in war-like accomplishments, in archery and casting the javelin, they judged him the most eager to learn and the most careful to practise. Again when he was old enough, he was most fond of hunting, ay and most ready to face danger among wild beasts. When a bear charged him once he did not shrink, but grappled with her; he was dragged off his horse, and received wounds which left their scars on him, but killed her at last; and he richly rewarded the first man who came to help.

Then he was sent down country as governor of Lydia and great Phrygia and Cappadocia, and appointed commander-in-chief of all the forces which had to assemble in the plain of Castolos. In this the first thing he made clear was, that if ever he made a truce or bargain or promise he never broke it. Indeed the cities put into his care all trusted him, and the men trusted him; and if anyone was an enemy, truce once made he trusted that nothing would be done to him contrary to that truce. Accordingly when he made war against Tissaphernes, all the cities willingly chose Cyros instead of Tissaphernes, except Miletos; and there the people feared him because he would not abandon their banished men. For he said, and he proved by his acts, that he never would abandon them when once he had become their friend, not even if they lost numbers and lost luck. If anyone did either evil or good to him, he tried to outdo them, and made that quite clear. Some said that his common prayer was, "May I live as long as I can go one better with friends and foes!" Indeed there was no man alive in our time who found so many others eager to grant him money and city and even their own bodies. To be sure, no-one could say that he allowed any to do harm or wrong and then laugh in his face; he punished quite without mercy, and you could often see by the highroads persons lacking feet or hands or eyes. The result was that in Cyros's province a man might travel fearlessly where he would, whether Hellene or Asiatic, and carry whatever suited him, so long as he did no wrong.

Moreover, those who were good men in war he rewarded

notably, as all agreed. For example, he had a war against the Pisidians and Mysians. He took the field himself against these countries; and when he saw men ready to take risks, he made these governors of the places he conquered, and rewarded them besides, and so these were seen to prosper exceedingly, and the cowards were thought fit to be their slaves. Therefore he found plenty of volunteers in any risk, when they thought Cyros would see.

In justice and honesty, if anyone showed himself glad to display these virtues, he took good care to make these richer than those who were greedy for unjust advantage. All his dealings were just, indeed, but he was especially particular to have a real army. Thus the captains and officers from abroad who served him for pay understood that to serve Cyros well was worth more to them than so much a month: besides this, if anyone did serve him well, he never left willing service unrewarded. Accordingly Cyros always found, as they said, the best men to carry out any enterprise.

If he saw one a skilful and just administrator, who managed his district well and collected the revenues, he never deprived him but always added to his trust; so men worked willingly, and got wealth boldly, and never tried to hide from Cyros what they got: he showed himself not one to envy those who were openly rich, but hidden riches he tried to bring into use. Friends again, if he made any and found them loyal, and judged them capable assistants in what he wanted to do, he treated well, no man better, as all agree. For just as he wanted friends to help in each undertaking, so he tried his best to help these friends in anything which he saw they wanted. More gifts were offered to him, I believe, than to any other man who ever lived, for many reasons; and no-one was ever more ready to distribute these among his friends, while he considered their tastes to see what each wanted most. When the gifts were meant for his person, whether in battle or just as finery, he used to say, "I can't deck out my body in all this finery, but a man's best finery is when his friends go fine."

In great things it is no wonder he could outdo his generous friends, since he had greater power; but he took care to have the better of them in little attentions and graces, which appears to me more admirable still. When he received some specially good wine, he would often send a keg half full to a friend, with a message, "I haven't drunk such good wine for a long time, so I send you this. Please drink it up to-day with your best friends!" Often he would send half a goose or half a cake, and things like that, telling his bearer to say, "Cyros liked this, and he wants you to have a taste." When hay was hard to get and he had plenty himself because he had provided it, and there were many servants, he would send round to tell his friends to stuff the horses they rode with this, that they might not starve while they carried his friends about. If he ever went on progress and crowds came to see him, he would call up friends and talk seriously to them, to show whom he valued.

So from all I hear, I judge that no-one has ever been better loved by Hellenes and Asiatics alike. Here is another proof. When Cyros was the king's slave, no-one ever left him for the king, only Orontas tried, and indeed the king himself found that the man he thought faithful to himself was a better friend to Cyros; but from the king, many did come away to Cyros after they became enemies, and those moreover whom the king cared for most—they thought that with Cyros if they played their parts well they would receive a worthier return than with the king. A great proof again is what happened at the end of his life, to show that he was noble himself, and knew how to judge rightly the trusty and loyal and firm; for when he died all his friends and table companions died fighting over him, except Ariaios, who was posted on the left wing, as it happened,

in command of the cavalry, and when he perceived that
Cyros was dead he escaped with all his command.

Then the head and right hand of Cyros were cut off. The
king, pursuing, fell on Cyros's camp; those with Ariaios
did not stand, but escaped through their own camp to the
stage-house where they had come from; the distance was
said to be four leagues. The king and his troops plundered
the camp, and took a great spoil, including the Phocaian
mistress of Cyros, famous as "the clever and beautiful."
The Milesian, who was younger, was caught by the king's
men, but she slipt out of her robe, and escaped to a body of
Hellenes who happened to be on guard among the baggage
animals. They resisted the plunderers and killed many of
them, and of themselves some were killed, too, yet they
did not take flight, but they saved the woman and everything else that was in their charge, goods and men.

At this time the king and the Hellenes were three or four
miles apart, the Hellenes pursuing and believing they were
victorious everywhere, the others plundering and believing
they were victorious themselves. But when the Hellenes
perceived that the king and his army were in their camp,
and when the king heard from Tissaphernes that the Hellenes were victors on their part and far away in pursuit, at
once the king collected his forces and put them in order.
Clearchos called Proxenos, who was nearest, and consulted
him whether they should send a party or all go back to
defend the camp.

Meanwhile the king showed himself advancing from the
rear, as it seemed. The Hellenes turned and prepared to
receive his attack on the spot, but the king did not approach
them; he passed them by the way he had come, outside
what had been their left wing, catching up those who had
deserted to the Hellenes in the battle, and also Tissaphernes
with his division. For Tissaphernes when they first met had
not taken flight, but he rode along the river through the Hel-

lenic targeteers; he killed none in passing through, but the Hellenes made room and struck at them and volleyed as they went. Episthenes of Amphipolis was in command, said to be a capable officer. Tissaphernes then got rather the worst of it but came out clear; he did not turn back, but went as far as to the Hellenic camp, and there found the king, when they put their forces together again and went on. When they came to the Hellenic left wing the Hellenes were afraid they might attack and surround them and cut them to pieces, and they decided to extend their line and put the river behind them.

While they were discussing this, lo and behold the king passed them, and placed his line opposite them in the same position as he was in at the beginning of the battle. When the Hellenes saw them near, and drawn up opposite, they chanted the battle-hymn again and charged much more vigorously than before. Again the barbarians would not stand, but ran even sooner than before.

The Hellenes pursued them as far as some village, and there they halted; for above the village was a mound, on which the king's party rallied, only cavalry now, but they covered the mound so that no-one could see what happened. But they said they did see the royal standard, a golden eagle, stretched across a shield and held up on a pole. As soon as the Hellenes moved again the horsemen at once left the mound, not all together but in small parties; the mound became bare by degrees, and at last they were all gone. Clearchos did not take his army upon the mound, but halted them at the foot, and sent up Lycios the Syracusan and one other to report what there was on the other side. Lycios rode up, and reported that they were all going as fast as they could.

Just then the sun set, the Hellenes halted and ordered arms, and rested, wondering why Cyros was nowhere to be seen and no messages came from him; for they did not know he was dead, but they supposed he was in pursuit, or gone forward to occupy some place. They deliberated whether they should stay there and bring up the baggage, or go back to camp. They decided to go back, and they reached the tents about supper-time.

This was the end of that day. They found most of their goods plundered, and all the food and drink gone; even the wagons loaded with barley and wine which Cyros had provided to distribute if the army were in special need (400 wagons, it was said), even these the king's army had spoiled. So most of the Hellenes had no dinner, and they had not had breakfast either; for the king appeared before the army was dismissed for breakfast. So they passed that night.

BOOK TWO

I

At daybreak the captains met. They were surprised that
Cyros had neither appeared himself, nor sent someone to
tell them what to do. They decided, therefore, to collect what
they had, and to get under arms, and to go on till they
found him. As they were just starting, at sunrise, up came
Procles, the governor of Teuthrania, a man descended from
Damaratos the Laconian,[1] and with him Glûs, the son of
Tamôs. These told them that Cyros was dead, but Ariaios
had escaped, and was with the other Asiatics in the stage-
house from which they marched on the day before; he said
he would wait that day for them, if they would come, but
on the morrow he was going back to Ionia, where he came
from.

When they heard this the captains were very much distressed, and so were the other Hellenes. Clearchos said,
"If only Cyros were alive! But pray report to Ariaios, that
we are victorious over the king, and, as you see, no-one is
left here to fight us; if you had not come, we should be
on the march against the king now. We say to Ariaios that

[1] a Spartan king deposed, who had settled in Mysia

if he will come here, we will place him on the royal throne; for the kingdom belongs to the conquerors."

With these words he sent the messengers away, and with them Cheirisophos the Laconian and Menon the Thessalian; Menon himself wished it, for he was a guest-friend of Ariaios.

So they went, and Clearchos remained. The army prepared food as well as they could, butchering the cattle and asses of the baggage train; they got wood by going a little in front of their lines, where they found plenty of arrows on the battlefield, which they had forced the deserters from the king to throw away, and the shields of wickerwork and Egyptian wooden shields. There were plenty of bucklers, too, and empty wagons which they could carry off. They used all these to boil the meat which they ate that day.

It was already about full-market time when messengers came from the king, heralds of the country, and one Hellene among them, Phalinos, who happened to be with Tissaphernes and highly respected; for he claimed to be expert in tactics and fighting in arms. These came and summoned the captains, and said, "The king having killed Cyros and won the victory, commands the Hellenes to lay down their arms, and find at the king's door what good they can."

Such was the king's message. The Hellenes were very angry, but Clearchos only said, "It is not for victors to lay down their arms." Then to the other captains, "You, my fellow-captains, answer these gentlemen as you think fairest and best; I will be here in a moment," for a servant had just called him to see the sacred parts which had been taken out from a victim which was being sacrificed. Then Cleanor the Arcadian, eldest of them, said they would die sooner than lay down their arms; and Proxenos the Theban said, "I wonder, Phalinos, whether the king speaks as conqueror or asks our arms as a friendly gift. If as conqueror, why does not he come and take them? If he wants us to yield them willingly, let him tell us what the soldiers will have left, if they make him a present of these?" Phalinos answered, "The king considers he is victor, since he has killed Cyros. For who is there who will challenge him for his empire? He considers that you also are his, because he holds you in the midst of his country, surrounded by impassable rivers, and he can bring against you such a multitude of men as you could not kill if you had the chance." Theopompos the Athenian followed and said, "My dear Phalinos, we have nothing good here, as you see, except arms and courage. While we keep our arms, we think we can use our courage; but if we give them up, we shall lose our lives too." Hearing this, Phalinos laughed, and said, "Why, you are quite a philosopher, young man, you speak neatly; but let me tell you that you are foolish if you think your courage can overcome the king's power." A few others, it is reported, showed a little weakness, and said they had been faithful to Cyros, and the king might find them valuable if he liked to be their friend; he might use them for a campaign into Egypt or something else, and they would go.

At this moment Clearchos returned and asked whether they had given their answer. Phalinos broke in, and said, "These people say all sorts of things, Clearchos; tell us what you say." He answered, "I was glad to see you, Phalinos, and so were the others, I think; you are a Hellene, and so are we, every one of us that you see before you. In our present case we ask your advice as to what we ought to do. Advise us in God's name what you think fairest and best, something that will do you honour when it is reported in time to come: how Phalinos was once sent by the king to command Hellenes to lay down their arms, and they asked his advice, and this was his advice. You know it is inevitable, that whatever you advise will be told all over Hellas."

Clearchos gave these hints hoping that the king's ambassador might advise them himself not to lay down their arms, and then the others would be more confident. But Phalinos did the opposite; he turned round, and said, "This is my advice. If you have one hope in ten thousand to make war against the king, and to save your lives, do not lay down your arms. But if there is no hope whatever of safety against the king's wish, I advise you to save yourselves in the one way you can." Clearchos answered to this, "Very well, that is what you say: from us take this answer. We believe that if we are to be friends to the king, we should be more valuable friends with arms than without; and if we are to make war, it is better to make war with arms than without." Phalinos said, "We will take back this answer; let me say that the king added, that there shall be a truce if you stay where you are, but if you move forwards or move backwards, war. Answer this too, then: will you stay, and is there a truce? Or shall I report that there is war?" "Report then," said Clearchos, "that our view is the same as the king's." "What does that mean?" said Phalinos. Clearchos answered, "If we stay where we are, a truce, if we move forwards or backwards, war." He asked again, "Truce or war, which?" Clearchos made the same answer again, "Truce if we stay here, war if we move forwards or backwards." But he did not indicate which he meant to do.

II

So Phalinos departed and those with him. Then Procles and Cheirisophos returned from Ariaios, but Menon stayed with him. These reported that Ariaios said there were many Persians better than himself who would never let him be king; "but if you wish to go away with him, he tells you to come to-night. Otherwise he says he will go early in the morning." Clearchos said, "Very good, so be it. If we come, then as you say; if not, do whatever you think most profitable for yourselves." But he did not tell these either what he meant to do.

After this, when the sun was already sinking, he called the captains and other officers together, and spoke to them.

"Gentlemen," he said, "I sacrifice for advance against the king, and the omens were not favourable. There is perhaps nothing strange in that; for between us and the king is the Tigris, a navigable river which we could not cross without boats, and boats we have none. However, we cannot stay where we are, for we cannot get provisions. But for going to the friends of Cyros the omens were completely favourable. This is what we must do. Dismiss, and dine on what we can find: when the first horn sounds for turning in, pack up; at the second, put the stuff on the animals; at the third, follow your guide, keeping the animals next to the river, and the shields outside." The captains and officers did so; and for the rest, he led and they followed—not that they chose him, but they saw that he alone understood what the leader ought to do, and the others were inexperienced.

After this, when darkness came, Miltocythes the Thracian deserted to the king, taking with him his horsemen, forty in number, and some three hundred of the Thracian footmen. Clearchos led the others as he had told them, and they followed, and they reached Ariaios and his force at the first stage-house, about midnight. They grounded arms in their ranks; and there was a meeting of the captains and other officers with Ariaios. The Hellenes and Ariaios and the chief of those with him swore to be allies and to be faithful to one another; the nationals also swore to lead the way honestly. This they swore, cutting the throats of a bull and a boar and a ram over a shield: the Hellenes dipt a sword in the blood, the Asiatics a spear. When the oath had been taken, Clearchos said:

"Now then, Ariaios, since the same journey is before us

all, tell me what notion you have of the road. Are we to return the same way as we came, or have you thought of another that seems better?"

He said, "If we go back by the way we came, we should perish of hunger outright; for we have no provisions now. Even on our way here we got nothing at all from the country on the seventeen last stages; where there was anything we have used it all up on the march already. The way we think of taking now is longer, but there will be no lack of provisions. We must make the first stages as long as we can, that we may get away from the royal army as far as we can; for if once we can put two or three days' journey between us, the king will never be able to catch us. With a small force he will not dare to follow; with a large force he will not be able to go fast, perhaps he will even fall short of provisions. That's my opinion," he said.

This plan of campaign meant nothing more than to cut and run; but fortune planned better.

When day came, they marched with the sun on their right hand, calculating that by sunset they would reach villages in the Babylonian country; and in this they were not deceived. But while it was still afternoon they thought they saw enemy horsemen; and those of the Hellenes who were not in their ranks fell in, and Ariaios (who was travelling in a wagon because he had been wounded) got down and put on his corselet, and so did those with him. While they were arming, their scouts came back reporting they were not cavalrymen but pack-animals grazing. And they soon understood that the king was encamped somewhere near, for smoke was seen in villages not far off. But Clearchos did not lead against the enemy, for he knew that the men were weary and hungry, and it was late already; yet he kept straight on without swerving, for he would not let them think he was running away, and at sunset he brought up his van to the nearest villages and encamped. From these everything had been stript by the royal army, down to the woodwork of the cottages. However, the first men encamped after a fashion, and those behind coming along in the dark lay in the open as it chanced, and they made a great noise calling to one another, so that even the enemy heard; and the nearest of the enemy even fled out of their encampment. This became clear next day; for not an animal was to be seen, no camp, no smoke anywhere near. The king himself was frightened, as it seemed, at the army's approach, as he made clear by what he did the day after.

However, as the night went on a panic fell on the Hellenes also and there was din and disturbance as one might expect in a panic. Clearchos sent round Tolmides the Elean, the herald who was with him as it happened, the best herald of his time; he was to call for silence, and proclaim from headquarters, one talent reward for information who let the ass loose in the camp. When this was proclaimed, the men knew that it was an empty panic and the commanders were safe and sound. At break of day Clearchos ordered the Hellenes to form in line in the same position which they had in the battle.

III

It was clear now that the king had been terrified by their approach, as I wrote above; for the day before he had commanded them to lay down their arms, but now at sunrise he sent heralds to treat for a truce. When they reached the outposts, these went in search of their commanders; and Clearchos, who happened to be then reviewing the lines, heard the report of the outposts, and sent back word that the heralds were to wait until he had leisure. When he had arranged his army so that a solid array could be easily seen everywhere, with no-one visible outside the forces, he summoned the mission, and went to meet them with the best armed and finest men he had, and told the other captains to do the same.

When he came up to the mission, he asked what they wanted. They answered that they came to arrange a truce, with full powers from the king to treat with the Hellenes, and to report their proposals to the king. Clearchos then said, "Report to him, then, that first there must be battle; we have no breakfast, and no man shall dare to speak of truce to Hellenes without providing breakfast." When the embassy heard this, they rode away, and soon came back; so it was plain that the king was somewhere near, or someone whose duty it was to arrange things. They said that the king thought it a reasonable request, and they had brought guides to take them where they would find breakfast, if they could arrange a truce. Clearchos asked whether the truce was offered just for the men as they went and came back, or was it a general truce for all. They replied, "For all, until we give our report to the king."

When they had finished, Clearchos removed them and held council; and it seemed best to accept this truce and quietly to go and get the provisions. So he said, "I agree with that, but I will not tell them at once; I will delay until the ambassadors are anxious for fear we may refuse to make truce. I think, however," he said, "that our own men will fear the same!" When he thought it was the right time, he announced that he would make truce, and bade them lead him at once to the provisions.

So they did; but Clearchos, although he had made the truce, marched with the army in battle order, himself commanding the rearguard. They came on ditches and canals full of water, which they could not cross without bridges; but they managed by making bridges of fallen date-palms or others which they cut down. Then one could learn what a commander Clearchos was. In his left hand he held the spear, a stick in his right; and if he thought there was any shirking, he picked out the right man and gave him one, and also he lent a hand himself, jumping into the mud, so that all were ashamed not to work as hard as he did. Those of thirty years and under were told off for this job; but when they saw how keen Clearchos was, the older men helped. What made him more anxious was that he suspected the ditches were not always so full of water, for it was not the season for watering the plain; he thought the king might have let in this water on purpose to show them how many dangers they would meet on the march.

At last they reached villages from which the guides directed them to take the provisions. There was plenty of corn and date-wine and a sour drink made by boiling dates. The palm-nuts or date-nuts which we see in our country are such as were kept for servants; but those reserved for the masters were select, wonderfully fine and large, just like amber in colour: and some they dry and store for delicacies. These were delicious as a relish for wine, but they give headache. That was the first time the men tasted the brain or top-cabbage of the palm, and most of them were surprised at the shape and peculiar flavour. This also was very apt to give headache. When the brain was taken from the palm, the whole tree withered.

There they remained three days. Then arrived Tissaphernes, and the queen's brother, and three other Persians, with a long train of slaves. When the Hellenic captains met them, Tissaphernes first spoke through an interpreter. He said:

"I am a near neighbour to Hellas, gentlemen; and when I saw you follow into danger and difficulty, I thought it a grand opportunity if I could persuade the king as a favour to let me bring you back safe to Hellas; for I think that would earn me your thanks and your country's. With this intention I put my petition before the king, saying that he

might fairly gratify me because I first told him that Cyros
was advancing against him, and I brought him aid along
with my news; and I alone of all those who faced the Hellenes did not take to flight, but I rode through and joined
the king in your camp which he had then reached, after
killing Cyros and pursuing the nationals with Cyros along
with the forces which are with me now, the most loyal of all
his men. He promised me that he would consider this; but
he told me to come and ask why you made war upon him.
And I advise you to answer moderately that it may be easier
for me to find how I may arrange something good for you."

The Hellenes retired and consulted what to say; and
they answered, Clearchos being spokesman:

"We did not assemble to make war on the king, nor did
we march against the king; but Cyros found many excuses,
as you know well yourself, that he might catch you unprepared and bring us here. However, when we saw him
in danger, we were really ashamed before gods and men
to desert him, after offering ourselves to him long since for
his service. But now that Cyros is dead, we do not lay claim
to the king's empire, and there is no reason why we should
damage the king's country or wish to kill the king himself.
We wish to march home, if no-one molests us; but if we
are injured we shall try to defend ourselves, with God's
help. If moreover, anyone turns up to help us, we shall be
no less ready to help him as far as we can."

Tissaphernes listened to him, and said, "I will report this
to the king, and bring back his answer. Until I return let
the truce be kept, and I will provide you a market." Next
day he did not return, and the Hellenes were anxious; but
he came the day after, and said he had procured from the
king the boon of safety for the Hellenes, although many
had urged that it was unworthy for the king to let go those
who had made war against him. At the end he said, "Now
you may receive our promise to keep the country at peace

with you, and to take you back to Hellas without fraud; we will provide a market, and wherever you cannot buy, we will allow you to take what is necessary from the country. You on your part must take your oath to march as through a friendly country, only taking food and drink without violence whenever we do not provide a market, but when we do you must buy provisions." This was agreed; they took the oath, and Tissaphernes and the queen's brother gave their right hands to the captains and officers of the Hellenes, and these did the like. After this Tissaphernes said, "Now, then, I return to the king; when I have arranged what I wish, I will come back ready to conduct you to Hellas, and myself to return to my province."

IV

After this the Hellenes and Ariaios waited for Tissaphernes, encamped near each other, for more than twenty days. Meanwhile Ariaios was visited by brothers and other relations, and some of his people had visits from Persians, who encouraged them, and brought pledges to some from the king, that the king would bear no malice against them for their campaign with Cyros or for anything else now bygone.

While this went on Ariaios's people clearly began to think less about the Hellenes. So for this reason they displeased many of the Hellenes; and these complained to Clearchos and the other captains, and said, "What are we waiting for? Don't we know that the king would give anything to destroy us, and show our whole nation what a terror it is to make war on the Great King? Now he deludes us to stay because his army is scattered; but when the whole army is assembled again there is no doubt he will attack us. Perhaps they are digging somewhere or fortifying somewhere to make the road impassable. He will never be willing, if he can help it, that we shall go back to Hellas and report that a few men like us beat the king in front of his own door, and got away to laugh at him."

Clearchos answered, "I have all this in my own mind, but I remember that if we go now he will think we have broken the truce and gone out for war. Then again, firstly no-one will make us a market or help us to get provisions; secondly, there will be no-one to guide us; thirdly, if we do anything like that Ariaios will leave us at once. So we shall not have one friend left, and even those who were friends will be our enemies. Then the river: if there is any other difficult river for us I don't know, but the Euphrates we know cannot be crossed if the enemy oppose. Further, we have no cavalry to help us if we must fight, but the enemy have plenty, and very good; so if we win, how could we kill anyone? And if we are beaten, none of us could escape. As for the king, with all these things in his favour, if he really wishes to destroy us, I don't know why we need swear oaths and give pledges, and then by perjury make his own word worthless to all the world, both ours and his!" He would often speak like this.

Meanwhile Tissaphernes came with his forces, as on the road home, and Orontas came with his; he brought also the king's daughter, his bride. They left the place at once, Tissaphernes leading and providing a market; Ariaios marched also at the head of Cyros's national force, along with Tissaphernes and Orontas, and camped with them. But the Hellenes suspected these, and kept to themselves with their own guides. They always camped with a distance between them, a league or more; both parties watched each other like enemies, and this at once made more suspicion. Sometimes when they were gathering wood from the same place, and foraging for grass and such things, they came to blows with each other, and this made more hostility.

After they had gone three stages they reached what is called the Wall of Media, and passed behind it. This was built of baked bricks set in asphalt, twenty feet thick, one hundred high; its length was said to be twenty leagues, and it is not far from Babylon. From this place they marched two stages, 8 leagues; and they crossed two canals, one by a bridge, one by eight boats fastened together. These canals came from the River Tigris; trenches are dug from them over the land, the first larger, then smaller ones, until at last they become little runnels such as we have in Hellas over millet fields.

Then they reached the Tigris, near which was a city, large and populous, named Sittace, distant from the river about a mile and a half. The Hellenes encamped near it beside a park, large and beautiful and thick with all sorts of trees; but the nationals crossed the river first, where they were quite hidden from view. After dinner it happened that Proxenos and Xenophon were walking in front of the camp, and a man asked the sentries where he could see Proxenos or Clearchos; he did not ask for Menon, although he came from Ariaios, Menon's friend. When Proxenos said, "I'm the man you are looking for," the fellow said, "I have been sent by Ariaios and Artaozos, who were true to Cyros and remain loyal to you. They bid you be on your guard against an attack to-night; there is quite an army close by in the park. And they bid you to send a guard for the Tigris bridge, because Tissaphernes intends to break it down to-night that you may not cross but may be caught between the river and the canal."

Hearing this they took him to Clearchos, and told him what he said. Clearchos was very much upset and alarmed. But a young man present observed that the attack and breaking down the bridge did not fit well together. "If they attack," he said, "they must either win or lose. If they win, why break down the bridge? For then we could never escape and be safe however many bridges there are. But if we win, with a broken bridge they will never escape themselves; nor will any of that multitude across the river be able to help them with a broken bridge." Clearchos listened, and asked the messenger how much country there was between the Tigris and the canal. He said a great deal, and many villages and many large cities. Then he understood at once that the Persians had sent the man, for fear the Hellenes might cut the bridge and stay in the island, defended by the Tigris on one side and the canal on the other, and might get their provisions from the country between, which was large and good with plenty of hands to till it; then again, it might be a refuge for anyone who wanted to damage the king.

After this they went to rest; however, they still sent a guard for the bridge. And no-one attacked them from any part, and none of the enemy came to the bridge, as the guards reported. But at dawn they crossed the bridge, which was made of thirty-seven vessels fastened together; they took all possible precautions, for some Hellenes from Tissaphernes brought word that they meant to attack while they were crossing. But this was false; however, as they were crossing Glûs appeared with some scouts to see if they were crossing the river, and when he saw he galloped away.

From the Tigris they marched four stages, 20 leagues, to the River Physcos, breadth 100 feet; there was a bridge across. There also was a large city, named Opis. There the Hellenes were met by the bastard brother of Cyros and Artaxerxes, from Susa and Ecbatana, bringing a large army to support the king; and halting his army he watched the Hellenes passing by. Clearchos led them two abreast, sometimes marching and sometimes halting. As long as the leading section of the army halted, so long there must be a halt through the whole army; so as the command ran down the whole army seemed to be enormous, even to the Hellenes themselves, and the Persian was dumbfounded at the sight.

Thence they marched through Media seven desert stages, 30 leagues, as far as the villages of Parysatis, the mother of Cyros and Artaxerxes. These Tissaphernes in mockery of Cyros gave over to the Hellenes to plunder, but no captives to be taken. There was plenty of corn there and sheep and other things. From there they marched four desert stages, 20 leagues, keeping the Tigris on the left. At the first stage beyond the river was an inhabited city named Cainai, large and prosperous, from which the natives used to bring over on rafts of skin, loaves, cheeses, and wine.

v

After this they reached the River Zapatas, breadth 400 feet. There they stayed three days; at this time there were suspicions, but no manifest plot. So Clearchos resolved to approach Tissaphernes, and see whether he could stop these suspicions before they brought war. He sent word that he wished to meet him, and Tissaphernes readily invited him to come. When they went Clearchos said:

"I know, Tissaphernes, that oaths have been sworn and pledges given between us that we will not harm each other; but I see you watching us like enemies, and we, seeing that, watch you too. But as by my inquiry I cannot perceive that you try to do us any hurt, and I know well that we never think even of such a thing, I thought it best to speak to you in hopes we may get rid of our mutual distrust. For I know it has often happened that either from slander or from suspicion men have been frightened of each other, and wishing to get in first before they suffer, they have done incurable mischief to others who were not intending to do anything of the sort, nor indeed wishing to do it. I think such misunderstandings are best ended by meeting face to face; so here I am, to assure you that you have no reason to distrust us. The first and chiefest thing is, that our oaths before heaven stop us from being enemies; I could never

deem one happy who knows he has disregarded his oath.
In war against heaven, what speed could save? What place
could be a refuge? How could one escape? What darkness
could he run to? What stronghold could receive him? All
things in every place are in God's hands, God equally rules
all. That is what I think about the oaths, and about the
gods before whom we made our pact of friendship and de-
posited it there; but of human things, I think at this present
you are the best thing we have. For with you every road
is easy, every river can be passed, there is no want of provisions. Without you every road goes through darkness,
for we know nothing about it; every river is hard to cross,
every crowd terrible, and most terrible of all the desert,
all full of want. If indeed we were so mad as to kill you,
by killing our benefactor should we not bring into the ring
against us that most mighty champion in reserve, the king
himself?

"Now for myself: let me tell you what high hopes and
prospects I should rob myself of, if I tried to do you any
harm. I wished Cyros to be my friend because I thought
him most able to benefit anyone he might wish; but you
I see now in his place. You hold the power and domain
of Cyros and keep your own besides; and the king's power,
which was Cyros's enemy, is your ally. This being so, who
is so mad that he does not wish to be your friend? Besides,
I will tell you reasons why I have some hope that you will
wish to be mine. I know the Mysians are a nuisance to
you, and I think I could make them humble with the force
I have here. I know about the Pisidians too; and there are
many other nations like that, which I think I could make
to cease from troubling your happiness. The Egyptians,
too, I understand you Persians are very angry with them;
and I don't see any force which could help you to punish
them better than this I now have. Then again, take your
own neighbours; if you wished to be a friend you could

be the greatest friend, and suppose anyone annoyed you, as master you might turn upon him if you had us to serve you, for we should serve you, not for the pay, but for the gratitude we should owe for saving us.

"When I think over all this in my mind it seems astonishing that you distrust us, and I would gladly hear you tell me by name who is an orator clever enough to persuade you that we are plotting against you."

Tissaphernes then answered the speech of Clearchos:

"Indeed I am glad, Clearchos, to hear your sensible words. For if that is your mind, I think you would be your own enemy as well as mine if you should plan mischief against me. Listen, and I will show you that you have just as little reason to distrust either the king or me. If we wished to destroy you, do you think we lack cavalry or infantry or armament, quite enough to damage you with no fear of suffering any harm in return? Then do you think there would be no suitable places for attack? Remember all the plains which you traverse with such hardship even while they are friendly. Look at all the mountains you must cross, which we could occupy before you and make impassable. Think of all the great rivers, where we can regulate our portions and decide how many we want to fight with. Some of them you could not possibly cross unless we ferried you over! Even if we should fail in all these, at least let me remind you, 'Fire is stronger than fruit'; we could burn up all the crops and enlist famine against you—however strong you are, you couldn't fight that!

"Then while we have so many ways to make war upon you, all without danger for ourselves, why should we choose the only way which is impious before heaven, the only way which is disgraceful before men? Men must be wholly helpless and resourceless and constrained by necessity, and they must be wicked too, if they are willing to use perjury to God and treachery to men in doing a thing. No, Clearchos, we are not so unreasonable or so foolish as that. Well, then, if we could destroy you, why did we not go so far? I assure you the reason was my passion to be trusted by the Hellenes. Cyros came up country trusting to this mercenary force, and I wished to go down again, made strong by benefits done to his same force. How you can be useful to me you have said, at least partly, but the greatest thing of all, I know: the tiara on the head only the king may wear upright, but the tiara on the heart perhaps with you to help another might find it easy to wear so."

Clearchos thought he spoke honestly, and he said:

"Then since we are such friends, those who try by calumny to make us enemies are worthy of death?" "Yes," Tissaphernes said, "and if your captains and your officers will come here, I will tell you openly who accuse you of plotting against me and my army." "Then I will bring them all," said Clearchos, "and I will reveal to you also where I hear this about you."

After this conversation Tissaphernes made a great fuss of him, and asked him to stay, and they dined together.

Next day when Clearchos came back to the camp it was clear that he thought himself great in friendship with Tissaphernes. He reported what he had said. "We must all go," he said, "as he asks, and any of us who are proved to be calumniating him, must be punished as traitors and enemies to us all." But he suspected the calumniator was Menon; for he knew that he and Ariaios had meetings with Tissaphernes, and that he was intriguing and scheming against himself in order to get command of the whole army and make himself a friend to Tissaphernes. Clearchos also wished that the whole army should follow his will, and that troublesome persons should be out of the way. But some of the soldiers protested that the captains and officers ought not all to go and trust Tissaphernes. But Clearchos insisted strongly, until he arranged that five captains should

go and twenty other officers; and about two hundred soldiers went with them to do their marketing.

When they reached the door of Tissaphernes the captains
were invited in, Proxenos the Bœotian, Menon the Thessalian, Agias the Arcadian, Clearchos the Laconian, Socrates
the Achaian; the other officers stayed at the door. A little
while afterwards, at one signal, those inside were seized,
and those outside were cut down. Soon after a number
of barbarian horsemen rode about the plain, and killed
every Hellene they met, slave or free. The men wondered
at this display of horsemanship from the camp, and did
not know what to make of it until a fugitive came in, Nicarchos, an Arcadian, wounded in the belly and holding his
bowels in his hands, and told what had happened. Then
all the Hellenes ran for their arms, all aghast, expecting they
would come to the camp instantly. They did not all come,
but Ariaios and Artaozos and Mithradates came, who had
been Cyros's most trusted friends; the interpreter of the
Hellenes said he saw and recognized the brother of Tissaphernes with them. They were attended by some three hundred Persians in corselets.

When these came near they called for any captain or
officer that they might deliver the king's message. After this
two captains came out, carefully guarded, Cleanor the
Orchomenian, and Sophainetos the Stymphalian, and with
them Xenophon the Athenian, who wished to hear news of
Proxenos; Cheirisophos happened to be absent in a village
with others getting provisions. When they stood within hearing, Ariaios said:

"Listen, Hellenes. Clearchos was shown to have perjured
himself and broken the truce; therefore he has been punished and he is dead; but Proxenos and Menon, because
they reported his plot, are in high honour. You lay down
your arms, that is the king's demand; he says they are his,
because they belonged to Cyros his slave."

The Hellenes made Cleanor their spokesman to answer, and he said, "You abominable wretch Ariaios, and you others who were friends of Cyros, have you no shame before gods and men? You swore the oath to have the same friends and enemies as we did, and you have betrayed us, with Tissaphernes, that most impious and godless villain! You have murdered the very man to whom you gave your oath, and you have betrayed us all, and you join our enemies to come against us!" Ariaios replied, "Because Clearchos was proved to have plotted first against Tissaphernes and Orontas, and against us all who are with them." Xenophon rejoined upon this, "Clearchos, then, is punished, if he broke the truce contrary to his oath, for the perjured are justly put to death, but what of Proxenos and Menon? They are your benefactors, and they are our captains, then send them here; for it is clear that being friends to both parties they will try to advise the best both for you and for us."

The barbarians discussed this for a long time, and then went away without answering a word.

VI

The captains, captured thus, were carried up to the king and there beheaded. One of them, Clearchos, was a true soldier and war was his passion, as all agreed who formed their opinions from personal knowledge. As long as the war lasted between Lacedaimon and Athens, he stayed at home; but when peace came he persuaded his own city that the Thracians were injuring the Hellenes; and having managed as well as he could with the ephors, he sailed to make war on the Thracians beyond Chersonese and Perinthos. However, the ephors changed their minds as soon as he had set out, and tried to turn him back from the Isthmus; but he would not obey them any longer, and sailed away to the Hellespont. Consequently he was sentenced to death by the Spartan government for disobedience to orders.

He was already a banished man when he came to Cyros. What arguments he used to persuade Cyros have been written elsewhere [1]; at least Cyros gave him 10,000 darics. He took the money, but he did not turn to a lazy life: no, with this money he collected a force and made war on the Thracians, and conquered them in battle; he ravaged them after that, and went on with the war until Cyros wanted his army—then he went off to make war again under him. These seem to me the doings of a man whose passion was war. When he could have kept at peace without shame or damage, he chose war; when he could have been idle, he wished for hard work that he might have war; when he could have kept wealth without danger, he chose to make it less by making war; there was a man who spent upon war as if it were a darling lover or some other pleasure.

So war was his passion; and he seemed a true soldier, because he loved perils; ready to lead against the enemy by day or by night, and he kept his head in danger, as those with him agreed one and all in every place. He had also the repute of a true leader, as far as was possible for a man of his character. He was able to think out ways to get provisions for his forces, and then to get them; and he was able to fix firmly in their minds that Clearchos must be obeyed. This he did by being severe; he was grim to look at and harsh in voice, he punished heavily and sometimes in anger, so that now and again he was sorry for it. And he punished on principle, for he thought an unpunished army was good for nothing; indeed, he used to say that a soldier ought to fear his commander more than the enemy, if he was to keep guard, or keep his hand off friends, or attack the enemy without excuses. In danger, however, the soldiers wished absolutely to obey him and chose no other; at such times his grimness appeared brightness, they said, his severity seemed strength against the enemy, so that they thought it salvation rather than severity. But when the danger was past,

[1] not known where

many left him if there was an opportunity to pass over to other commanders; for he had no charm, and he was always severe and cruel, so the soldiers felt towards him as boys towards a schoolmaster. Indeed, he never found any to follow him for affection and friendship; but those who were put under his charge by some authority, or through need or some other constraint, he found completely obedient. But when they began to succeed in conquering an enemy under him, his men had strong motives to make them useful; for one thing, they felt confident of victory, and for another they feared punishment from him, which made them obedient.

Such was Clearchos as a commander; but it was said he did not like very much to be commanded himself. He was about fifty years old when he died.

Proxenos the Bœotian ever since the days of his youth had longed to become a man capable of doing great things; and because of this longing he paid his fees to Gorgias of Lentinoi.[1] After being with Gorgias he thought himself at once quite capable of being a ruler, and since he was a friend of the first men of his day he thought himself the equal of any man as a benefactor. In this spirit he took part in the business of Cyros; he believed he should get a great name from this, and great power and wealth. Yet although he longed so much for these great things, all the same it was quite clear that he did not wish to get any of them by injustice; with justice and honour he thought these things ought to be got, but not without. To rule gentlemen he was well able, but still he could not put fear or respect for himself into his soldiers. Indeed, he had rather respect for the soldiers than they had for him, and he obviously feared rather to be disliked by the soldiers than the soldiers feared to disobey him. He thought that to praise one who did well, and not to praise the offender, was enough to make a ruler and the reputation of a ruler. Therefore the gentlemen

---

[1] the rhetorician, who asked 100 minae

among his associates liked him and wished him well, but common men schemed against him and thought him easy game. When he died, he was about thirty years old.

There was no doubt about Menon the Thessalian [1]; it was obvious that he desired with all his heart to be rich, that he desired to rule in order that he might get more, that he desired to be honoured in order that he might make more profit. He wished to be friend to the most powerful that he might do wrong and not be punished. He believed that the shortest way to accomplish what he desired was perjury and lying and deceit, but simplicity and truth were just foolishness. It was clear that he had affection for no-one, but he obviously plotted against any he called friend. He never laughed at an enemy, but he always talked as though he was laughing at all his associates. He had no designs against the possessions of his enemies, for he thought it was difficult to get hold of things well guarded; but he believed he was the sole discoverer how easy it is to get hold of the unprotected, that is, what his friends had. If he found out that any were perjured and dishonest, he feared them as being well armed; but pious men, and those who practised truth, he tried to use as being cowards. As others pride themselves on godliness and truth and honesty, so Menon prided himself on his power to deceive, to fabricate falsehoods, to mock at his friends. If a man was not unscrupulous he always thought him one of the uneducated. If he wanted to make himself first in the friendship of any, he thought it should be done by slandering those who were first. To make his soldiers obedient, his principle was to share in their misdeeds; he expected to be honoured and courted if he showed that he would and could do most in that line. If ever anyone held aloof, he called it a real kindness that he had not destroyed him while they were friends. There are indeed certain obscure charges against him which may not be true, but here are some things which everyone knows.

[1] This is again Plato's Menon, who is a happier figure in those pages.

He was in the bloom of his youth when he got command
of the mercenaries from Aristippos; he became very intimate with Ariaios, who was a barbarian, because the man
liked handsome lads; he himself, while yet beardless, had
a bearded favourite in Tharypas. When his fellow-captains
were put to death for marching with Cyros against the
king, he was not put to death although he had done the
same; but after the death of the others he was punished with
death by the king, not beheaded like Clearchos and the rest,
which is thought to be the quickest death, but it is said kept
alive for a year and tortured until he died the death of a
malefactor.

Agias the Arcadian and Socrates the Achaian were also
put to death. No-one had a bad word to say of these, either
as soldiers or as friends. Both were about five-and-thirty
years of age.

BOOK THREE

I

After the captains had been seized, and the officers and men who were their escort had been cut down, the Hellenes were in despair, full of anxiety. There they were at the king's door, and round them everywhere so many nations and cities of the enemy. No-one now would provide them a market; they were distant from Hellas more than a thousand miles, with no guide for the road. Impassable rivers crossed the homeward way, and they had been deserted even by the natives who had come up country with Cyros. They were left alone without one single horseman to help them, so that it was clear that if they were victorious they could kill no-one, and if they were worsted not one of them would be left. These thoughts passed through their minds and made them spiritless. Few of them tasted food that evening, few lit a fire; many of them never came into camp that night, but they rested each where he chanced to be. They could not sleep for sorrow, longing for home and parents, for wives and children, which they never expected to see again. In this state they all tried to rest.

There was in the army an Athenian, Xenophon, who

came with them neither as captain nor officer nor man, but Proxenos had invited him to come, being an old family friend. Proxenos promised, if he would come, to introduce him to Cyros, who was, he said, more than home and country to himself. Xenophon read his letter, and consulted Socrates the philosopher about this trip. Socrates had a suspicion that there might be some state objection to his being friendly with Cyros, because Cyros had favoured the Lacedaimonians in their war against Athens; so he advised Xenophon to go to Delphi and inquire of the oracle about this journey. Accordingly Xenophon went and asked Apollo what god he should sacrifice and pray to, that he might best accomplish the journey he had in mind, and come back safe and successful. Apollo named the gods to whom he must sacrifice.

When he came back he told the oracle to Socrates. But Socrates blamed him because he had not asked first whether it was better for him to go or to stay, but just decided to go, and then asked how he could best do it. "But," said he, "since you did ask that, you must do what the god bids." So Xenophon sacrificed to those gods as he was directed, and set sail; and at Sardis he found Proxenos and Cyros on the point of going up country, and then he was introduced to Cyros. Proxenos urged him to stay, and Cyros urged him too, and promised he would send him home as soon as the campaign was over. The expedition was said to be against the Pisidians; and so he joined it, being thus deceived—but not by Proxenos, for he did not know of the attack to be made upon the king, nor did anyone else of the Hellenes except Clearchos.

However, when they got as far as Cilicia, it seemed to be clear to all that they were marching against the king. Most of them followed for shame of one another and Cyros, although they feared the journey and went against their will; and one of these was Xenophon.

And now in their desperate plight, he was unhappy like the rest and could not sleep; but he did snatch a nap, and then he saw a dream. He thought there was lightning and a thunderbolt fell on his father's house, and all was in a blaze. He woke at once in terror; the dream he judged to be good in one way, because amid troubles and dangers he seemed to see a great light from Zeus, but in another way he feared, because he considered the dream to come from Zeus the king and the blaze of fire seemed to be all round, so he feared difficulties would fence him in all round, and he might not be able to get out of the country of the king. But what such a dream really means may be seen from what happened afterwards; and this is what happened.

As soon as he was awake, the first thought that came into his head was, "Why do I lie here? The night is going on, and with daylight it is likely the enemy will come. If we fall into the power of the king, now we must see the most cruel sights, and feel the most terrible pains, and die by violence—and how can it be helped? But how are we to defend ourselves? No-one is preparing for that, no-one cares about that, but we lie here as if it were possible to live in peace and quiet! What about me then? What captain from what country do I expect to do that? Am I waiting till I grow old enough myself—and how old? I shall never be any older at all, if I give myself up to the enemy to-day."

Then he got up, and first called together the under-officers of Proxenos. When they were collected he said:

"Gentlemen, I cannot sleep and I don't think you can; and I can't lie here when I see what a plight we are in. It is clear that the enemy did not show us open war until they thought they had everything well prepared; and no-one among us takes the pains to make the best possible resistance.

"Yet if we give way, and fall into the king's power, what

do we expect our fate will be? When his own half-brother was dead, the man cut off his head and cut off his hand and stuck them up on a pole. We have no-one to plead for us, and we marched here to make the king a slave or to kill him if we could, and what do you think our fate will be? Would he not go to all extremes of torture to make the whole world afraid of making war on him? Why, we must do anything to keep out of his power! While the truce lasted, I never ceased pitying ourselves, I never ceased congratulating the king and his army. What a vast country I saw, how large, what endless provisions, what crowds of servants, how many cattle and sheep, what gold, what raiment! But when I thought of these our soldiers—we had no share in all these good things unless we bought them, and few had anything left to buy with; and to procure anything without buying was debarred by our oaths. While I reasoned like this, I sometimes feared the truce more than the war now.

"However, now they have broken the truce, there is an end both to their insolence and to our suspicion. There lie all these good things before us, prizes for whichever side prove the better men; the gods are the judges of the contest, and they will be with us, naturally. These men are perjured before them, while we saw so many good things and kept strictly away from them because of our oaths sworn to the gods; therefore we may enter the contest, it seems to me, with much better hearts than they can.

"Besides, our bodies are better fitted than theirs for bearing cold and heat and hardship; and our souls are better, thank God! They are men easier to wound and to kill than we are if the gods give us victory as before.

"Perhaps others are now thinking the same, but in heaven's name don't let us wait for someone else to come and pat us on the back and say, Go it. Here's a grand enterprise! Let us take the lead and show the others how to be brave!

Show yourselves the best of officers, and as worthy to be captains as the captains themselves! Count on me, if you are willing to make the start; I will follow you, or if you order me to lead, I will not make my youth an excuse, but I think I am old enough to keep danger from myself!"

The officers on hearing this address all asked him to be their leader, except a certain Apollonides who spoke in the Bœotian dialect. He said it was all nonsense to pretend that any safety could be found except with the king's consent, if that could be had, and at the same time he began to speak of the difficulties. But Xenophon cut him short and said:

"Man, I'm amazed at you! You have eyes to see, but you understand not; you have ears to hear, but you remember not! You were there with the others, I think, when the king was so proud after the death of Cyros, and sent to demand our arms. We refused to give them up, but went and encamped beside him. What didn't he do! Sent ambassadors, asked for a truce, gave provisions till he got it! And when the captains and officers did what you tell us to do, and went for a conference without arms, trusting to this truce—where are they now? Beaten, stabbed, insulted, the poor devils can't even die, though that is what they long for! And you know all this, and you say those who urge resistance are talking nonsense, and you tell us to go there again and try persuasion! In my opinion, men, we ought not to let this man be one of us. We ought to take his rank from him, and put a pack on his back, and make him carry for us. This man is a disgrace to his own country and to all Hellas, because he is a Hellene and yet behaves like this."

Then Agasias the Stymphalian broke in and said:

"But this fellow has nothing to do at all with Bœotia or Hellas; I have noticed that both his ears are bored, like a Lydian's." And so they were; accordingly they drove him away.

The others went the rounds; wherever a captain was in

some post they called him along, wherever there was none, the second-in-command, or where a lieutenant was left alive the lieutenant.

When all were collected they seated themselves in front of the place of arms; they were about one hundred captains and other officers.

It was about midnight now. Then Hieronymos of Elis, the eldest of Proxenos's officers, began to speak. He said:

"Gentlemen, captains and officers of our army, seeing the state we are in we thought it best to meet and to invite you, that we might devise some good plan amongst us. I call on you, Xenophon, to speak as you did to us."

Then Xenophon said:

"Well, we all know that the king and Tissaphernes have seized all of us they could, and it is clear they are planning to destroy us if they can. My opinion is that we ought to do anything and everything not to fall into the power of these barbarians, but turn the tables on them. Let me point out to you, then, that you now here assembled have a grand opportunity. All these soldiers have their eyes on you. If they see you are discouraged they will all be cowards; but if you show that you are making preparations against the enemy, and if you call on them, you may be sure they will follow you and try to imitate you. Perhaps it is fair to expect you to be a bit better than they are. You are captains, you see, or you are in command of troops and companies, and while there was peace, you had more wealth and honour; then now when war has come, we must ask you to be better than the mob, and to plan and labour for their behalf, if necessary.

"Now, first of all, I think you will do the whole army a great service if you take care at once to appoint captains and officers in the place of those who have been lost. For it is true one may say universally that without commanders nothing good or useful could ever be done: good discipline always saves, but disorder has destroyed many. When you have appointed as many commanders as are wanted, assemble all the other soldiers and encourage them; that will be just what they want now. Perhaps you have noticed yourselves how crestfallen they were when they came into camp, how crestfallen they went on guard; in such a state I don't know what you could do with them, either by night or by day. But if someone could turn their minds from wondering what will happen to them, and make them wonder what they could do, they will be much more cheerful. You know, I am sure, that not numbers or strength brings victory in war; but whichever army goes into battle stronger in soul, their enemies generally cannot withstand them.

"I have noticed also myself, gentlemen, that when men seek for nothing in warfare but only life at all costs, they are generally the ones to die, and that with disgrace and ignominy; but when they recognize that all men must die, for this is their common lot, and strive only to die with honour, these I generally see growing to old age, and while they live, much happier. Learn this lesson yourselves, for now is the time we need it: be men yourselves, and encourage others to do the same."

With these words he sat down; and after him Cheirisophos rose and said:

"All I knew of you before, my dear Xenophon, was just that I heard you were an Athenian; but now I admire you for what you say and what you do, and I wish there were many more like you—that would be a public benefit. And now, gentlemen," he went on, "don't let us waste time; dismiss and choose commanders, those who need them, then come back here to the middle of our camp, and bring the selected men. After that, we will summon all the troops to a meeting there. And we must have Tolmides the herald there too." As he said this he got up and went to do what was necessary without delay. Then officers were chosen: in place of

Clearchos, Timasion the Dardanian; in place of Socrates, Xanthicles the Achaian; in place of Agias, Cleanor the Arcadian; in place of Menon, Philesios the Achaian; in place of Proxenos, Xenophon the Athenian.

II

When these had been elected it was almost dawn, and the commanders came forward. They decided to set the watch and to convene the men. When the soldiers were all there, first Cheirisophos the Lacedaimonian got up and spoke as follows:

"Soldiers, this is a dangerous time, when we have lost such captains and officers and men; and besides, our former allies, Ariaios and his men, have betrayed us. But we must face the dangers, and prove good men, and not give in, but try to save ourselves by a handsome victory if we can. If not, at least let us die with honour, but let us never fall into our enemies' hands alive; for I think we should suffer such things as the gods would do to their enemies."

After him Cleanor the Orchomenian rose and said:

"You see, men, the king's perjury and impiety! You see the treachery of Tissaphernes! He said he was near neighbour to Hellas, and would do so much to save us, he swore solemn oaths to us himself, he gave us pledges himself, and then he deceived us himself—seized our captains, feared not the God of Guests, but invited Clearchos to sit at his table, and then made this very act the means of destroying those men! Ariaios again—we would have made him king, we gave and received pledges to be true to each other, but he did not fear God. Cyros alive honoured him highly, but he had no respect for Cyros dead; now he has deserted to the bitterest enemies of Cyros, and tries to ruin the friends of Cyros! These men may the gods punish; but we, seeing this, must not be deceived by these men again. We must fight our strongest, and leave our fate in the hands of the gods."

Then Xenophon rose; he was arrayed for war in his finest dress. "If the gods grant victory," he thought, "the finest adornments are most proper for such a victory; if I must die, after grand ambitions I would meet my end in grandeur." Then he began as follows:

"The perjury and treachery of the barbarians Cleanor has spoken of, and I think you know it yourselves. Then if we wish to be friends with them again, we must feel very much disheartened when we see what our captains have suffered when they trusted themselves to them in good faith. But if we have in mind to punish them in arms for what they have done, and to be henceforth in war with them out and out, then with God's help there are many good hopes of safety."

While he was speaking someone sneezed [1]; the soldiers hearing this, kissed their hands to heaven, and Xenophon said:

"While we were speaking of safety came an omen of Zeus the Saviour! Then I think we should vow to this god a thanksgiving for salvation as soon as we reach the first friendly country, and vow a sacrifice to the other gods according to our ability. Whoever agrees with this, let him hold up his hand."

All held up their hands. Then they made their vow and chanted the battle-hymn. After this matter of piety was settled he began again:

"I am just saying that we have many good hopes of safety. Firstly, we abide by our solemn oaths; but the enemy have perjured themselves and broken the truce contrary to their oaths. It is reasonable, then, that the gods should be against our enemies and should be our own allies; and they are able quickly to make the great small, and easily to save the small in time of danger, if it be their pleasure. Next I will remind you of the dangers which our ancestors faced, and you will see that it is proper for you to be good men, and that good

---

[1] a good omen

men are saved with the gods' help even from great danger.

"The Persians came, you know, with their enormous fleet, to wipe out Athens; but the Athenians dared to stand up to them and conquered them. They had vowed to Artemis to sacrifice as many goats as they should kill Persians; but they could not find enough, so they resolved to sacrifice every year five hundred, and they do so still. Again later, when Xerxes collected that innumerable host against Hellas, then again our ancestors conquered the ancestors of these men by land and sea. We can see proofs of this in the trophies, but the greatest proof is the freedom of those cities in which you were born and brought up; for you revere no man as master, but only the gods.

"Such were your ancestors. I will not say indeed that you are not worthy of them. No, not many days ago you faced these their descendants, many times your number, and conquered them. Then you did your part well, in order to make Cyros king; now that your own life and safety is at stake, I take it you ought to be much better and much more resolute. Moreover, you must be more confident against your enemy. At that time you had no experience of them, yet you dared to attack them with the spirit of your fathers. Now you have found by experience that they will not stand up to you even if they are many times your number. Then why should you fear them? And pray consider it no great loss that Cyros's men who stood by us once have left us. For they are greater cowards than those whom you beat; at least they took refuge with them when they left us. If people want to be in the front ranks of a flight, I prefer to see them in our enemies' ranks rather than in ours.

"If any of you is downhearted because we have no cavalry but the enemy have many, remember that their ten thousand cavalry are only ten thousand men. No-one ever died in battle from the kick or the bite of a horse; the men make them do whatever they do in battle. In fact, we have a safer carrier than cavalry; there they hang on their horses fearing a fall as well as a foe, but we stand on the ground, and we can hit harder if anyone attacks, and aim better. The cavalry have indeed one advantage; they can cut and run more safely!

"Perhaps you feel bold enough about battle, but you are anxious because Tissaphernes will not guide us any longer and the king will not provide a market. Think a moment whether it is better to have Tissaphernes for a guide, when he is clearly planning mischief against us, or any men we can catch to make them guide us; they know that if they do us wrong, their lives and bodies are at stake. And provisions: is it better to buy from the market which those men provided, small measure for big price, when we have not even the price now; or to take it ourselves if we beat them, with any measure we like?

"Perhaps you recognize we are better off as it is, but think the rivers an impassable obstacle; you consider you have been badly deceived when you crossed them. But think whether this is not really the most foolish thing which the barbarians have done. All rivers are passable when you come near the source, hardly knee-deep, although they may be impassable far down. But assume that the rivers will not let us across and no guide can be found, even so we must not lose heart. Look at the Mysians; we should not say they are better than we are, but we know there are many large and prosperous cities full of them, in the king's country, without his leave. We know the same of Pisidians, and we have seen ourselves that Lycaonians have seized the strong places in the plains and reap his country. So with us: I think we ought not to show that we have set out for home, but make preparations to live here. I know quite well that the king would give plenty of guides to the Mysians, and hostages for honest dealing, and he would make roads for them even if they wished to depart in four-horse chariots. Be sure he would think himself thrice blessed to do it for us, if he saw us preparing to settle down! But I am afraid that if we once learn to live idle in luxury, and to dally with the fine big women and girls of the Medes and Persians, we may be like the lotus-eaters and forget the way home!

"I think, then, that we must first try to reach Hellas and our own people, and show the Hellenes that they are poor only because they want to be, when they could bring their paupers over here and see them rich. But don't forget, men, that all these good things belong to the conquerors; and now it is necessary to say how we can travel most safely and fight most successfully.

"First of all, then, I propose that we burn the wagons we have, that the baggage-train may not be our captain, and we may go where is best for the army. Next, burn the tents too: for these are a nuisance to carry, they don't help us to fight or to find provisions. Further, let us get rid of superfluous baggage, keeping only what we need for battle or eating or drinking; so the greatest number of us will be under arms, and as few as possible carrying baggage. You know, of course, that if we are beaten, someone else owns all our goods; if we win, we may call the enemy our porters.

"It remains to say what I think is the chief thing of all. You see that the enemy dared not make war upon us until they had seized our leaders. They believed that while the commanders were there, and while we obeyed, we were able to defeat them; when they took our commanders, they thought we should be destroyed by anarchy and disorder. Very well: the commanders must be much more careful than before, and the commanded must be more obedient than before: and if anyone disobeys, we must vote that each and all of you must help the commander to punish.

So the enemy will find themselves mightily mistaken: for this day they will see ten thousand Clearchoses instead of one, who will never permit anyone to be a coward.

"But now it is high time for me to finish; perhaps the enemy will be here soon. Then let those who think I am right support me at once, that my proposals may be carried out. Or if anyone has anything better, let him speak up boldly and say so, even if he is a private soldier, for our common safety is our common need."

After this Cheirisophos said, "If we need anything else, beside what Xenophon says, we can do it by and by; but I think it best to carry these proposals at once. Whoever agrees, let him hold up a hand." All held up their hands. Then Xenophon rose again and said, "Men, listen to something else I have to propose. It is clear that we must march where we can find provisions, and I hear there are good villages not more than ten miles away. Then we should not be surprised if the enemy follow us when we go, as cowardly dogs chase and bite those who pass, if they can, but run away if they pursue. Then it is safe perhaps to march in a hollow square, with the armed men outside and the baggage and crowd of camp followers safer in the middle. Suppose we decide who is to lead the square, and keep order in front, and who is to be on the flanks, and who to bring up the rear, we shall not have to consider when the enemy come, but we can just use the arrangements. If anyone sees anything better, let us do as he says: otherwise let Cheirisophos lead the van, since he is a Lacedaimonian, and the two eldest captains see to the flanks; while the youngest, I and Timasion, will take the rear for the present. We will just try this arrangement, and for the future we can do as may seem best. If anyone has a better plan, let him speak." As no-one spoke, he said, "Those in favour, hold up a hand." All agreed. "Now then," he said, "dismiss and do it as agreed. And if any of you wants to see his dear ones again, let him remember to be a true man, for that's the only way to do it. Whoever wants to live, let him try to conquer, for the conquerors kill and the conquered die. If anyone wants riches, let him try to win; for conquerors preserve their own and take the goods of the conquered."

III

After these harangues, they went and burnt the wagons and tents; superfluous things they gave to any who wanted them, and threw the rest into the fire. This done, they took breakfast.

While they were at breakfast, up came Mithradates with about thirty horsemen, and, calling the captains within hearing, he spoke as follows:

"I was faithful to Cyros, as you know, Hellenes, and now I am friendly to you; indeed I spend my days here in great fear. So if I saw that you had some profitable plan for safety, I would join you with all my servants. Tell me, then, what you have in mind, and regard me as a friend and well-wisher, willing to make my journey along with you."

The captains consulted, and decided to answer this, with Cheirisophos as spokesman: "We are resolved to pass through the country doing as little damage as possible, if we are left alone; but if anyone tries to hinder our march, we will fight him as stoutly as we can." After this Mithradates tried to show them that it was impossible to save their lives except with the king's consent. Then it became clear that he was a spy; for one of the relations of Tissaphernes was there to keep him loyal. After this the captains thought it best to proclaim war without parley for as long as they were in the enemy country; for they used to come and try to corrupt the soldiers, and they did corrupt one officer, Nicarchos the Arcadian, who deserted at night with about twenty men.

After this, they breakfasted and crossed the Zapatas River;

then began their march in order, with baggage and mob in the middle. They had not gone very far when Mithradates appeared again with some two hundred horsemen and bowmen and slingers, four hundred or so, very light and trim. He came towards them in friendly fashion, but when they were near suddenly there were arrows from both horse and foot, and the slingers too wounded many. The Hellenic rearguard suffered severely but could do nothing in return: for the range of the Cretan bowmen was less than the Persian, and besides being bare they had to be inside the defences, and the slingers were beyond the range of their javelins.

So Xenophon ordered pursuit, and the men-at-arms and targeteers of his rearguard did pursue, but they caught none of the enemy. For the Hellenes had no horsemen, and the footmen could not catch the enemy footmen with a long start in a short run; of course they could not go far from the army, and the barbarian horsemen shot arrows behind them as they rode and hit them, besides they had to come back all that way fighting. The result was that they made no more than three miles or so in all that day, but towards evening they reached the villages.

Then again there was great discouragement. Cheirisophos and the older captains blamed Xenophon because he left the lines to pursue, and risked himself but could do no harm to the enemy. Xenophon listened, and said they were quite right in blaming him, as the result had showed. "But I was compelled to pursue," he said, "when I saw that we suffered so badly by standing still and we could do nothing in return. When we did pursue, what you say is the truth," says he; "we could do them no damage, and got back with great difficulty. Thank God they had only a small force, so they could not hurt us seriously, but they showed us what we want. Their arrows and slings have such a range that the Cretans cannot reach them, nor those who throw by hand; and when we pursue, it is impossible to go far from our army, and in a short space not even a fast runner could catch a runner with a bowshot start. Well, then, if we are to keep them from damaging us on the march, we must find slingers and horsemen at once. I hear there are Rhodians in the army, and most of them know how to sling, as they say, and their shot has twice the range of the Persians. The Persians use a stone as big as your fist, and so they cannot throw far, but the Rhodians know how to use leaden bullets. If we can discover, then, which of them possess a sling and pay them extra for this, and pay for plaiting more slings, and invent some other privilege for those willing to be posted as slingers, perhaps we shall find some useful men. I see also that there are horses with us; I have some myself, some were left by Clearchos, many others which we captured are carrying baggage. If we take the pick of these, and put other animals to carry, we can use the horses for cavalry, and perhaps these will do damage in the pursuit."

This was agreed to; and that night about 200 slingers were found up, and the next day some 50 horses and horsemen were passed as fitting, and buff jackets and corselets were provided for them, and Lycios the Athenian, Polystratos' son, was put in command of the horse.

IV

They stayed there that day, and on the next began the march earlier than usual, for they had to pass through a ravine where they feared the enemy might attack them in the pass. When they had passed, Mithradates appeared again with 1,000 cavalry and some 4,000 bowmen and slingers. He had demanded so many from Tissaphernes, and promised that if he got them he would deliver the

Hellenes into his hand: he despised them because in the former attack with a small force he had done much damage, as he thought, and suffered nothing at all.

When the Hellenes had gone about a mile from the pass, Mithradates came through with his force. Orders had been given which of the targeteers and men-at-arms were to pursue, and the horsemen were told to pursue boldly and a sufficient force would follow. So when Mithradates caught them up, and arrows and slingstones began to come, a trumpet sounded for the Hellenes, and the appointed parties doubled out at once and the horsemen galloped; the enemy did not wait for them but ran back into the ravine. In this pursuit, many of the barbarians were killed, and some of the cavalry were taken alive, about eighteen. The dead bodies were mutilated by the Hellenes unbidden, to strike terror into the enemy.[1]

But the enemy retired after this, and the Hellenes marched unmolested the rest of the day as far as the River Tigris. A large deserted city was there, named Larisa,[2] which had once been inhabited by Medes. The wall of this place was five-and-twenty feet thick, and one hundred high, the whole being two leagues round. It was built of clay bricks, on a stone base twenty feet high. When the Persians took the empire from the Medes the Persian king besieged this place and could not take it in any way; then a cloud covered the sun and hid it until the people escaped, and so it was taken. Near this city was a stone pyramid, one hundred feet wide and two hundred high. On this pyramid were many of the natives who had escaped from the villages near.

From this place they marched one stage, 6 leagues, to a large deserted fortress named Mespila,[3] formerly inhabited by Medes. The foundation was made of polished stone full of shells, fifty feet wide and fifty high; the circuit was 6 leagues. There the king's wife Medeia[4] is said to have taken refuge when the Medes lost their empire to the Persians.

---

[1] They only imitated the Persian custom.
[2] modern Nimrud
[3] Calah, or Nineveh. The first Cyros took it in 558 B.C.
[4] wife of Astyages, the last King of Media

The Persian king besieged this place, but could not take it either by time or by force; but Zeus affrighted the inhabitants by thunder, and so it was taken.

From this place they marched one stage, 4 leagues. On this stage Tissaphernes appeared, with his own cavalry and the forces of Orontas, who married the king's daughter, and the nationals whom Cyros had brought up country with him, and those whom the king's brothers had brought to support the king; it so appeared to be an immense army. When he was near he stationed some ranks in the rear, and led others along the flanks, but he dared not attack and he wished to run no risk, only gave orders to shoot with bow and sling. But the Rhodians posted here and there slung their bullets and the bowmen shot their arrows, and not one missed a man (he would have found it hard to miss if he had tried); so Tissaphernes quickly retreated out of range, and the other ranks retreated too. For the rest of the day they went on marching, and the barbarians did no harm by their sharpshooting; for the Rhodians had longer range than the Persians, even the bowmen. The Persian bows are very large; so the arrows they picked up were useful to the Cretans, who practised with them, shooting high and as far as possible. Plenty of gut was found in the villages, and lead, which they used for the slings.

So on this day, after the Hellenes had encamped in villages which they found, the barbarians had the worst of that skirmish, and retreated. The day following the Hellenes spent in the villages collecting provisions, for there was plenty of corn there. Next day they marched on over the plain, and Tissaphernes followed, skirmishing. Now the Hellenes discovered that the square was a bad formation with the enemy following. If the wings of the square draw together when the road is narrow, or where the hills make it necessary, or a bridge, the armed men must be greatly distressed and march badly; they are squeezed up and disordered at the same time, so they are not easy to manage because they lose discipline. Again, when the wings open again after their late distress, the ranks must be separated again, and there are empty spaces between, and all are discouraged with an enemy behind. Or if they have to cross a bridge or some other crossing, each man tries to get over first, and then it is easy for the enemy to attack.

When the commanders perceived this they made six companies of a hundred men each, and appointed a lieutenant to command each, and officers for each half-company and quarter-company.[1] When the wings drew in on the march these companies fell to the rear so as not to confuse the wings, and they lined up outside the wings. When the wings expanded again they filled up the gap in the line between, in line of companies in column if narrow, half-companies if wider, quarter-companies very wide, and so the gap was always filled. Thus they were not disordered if they had to cross a ford or a bridge, but the companies crossed in turn; and when they needed the line these were ready.

In this way they marched four stages. While they were in the fifth they saw a palace and many villages round it, but the road to this led amongst high foothills rolling down from the mountains under which the village lay. The Hellenes were glad indeed to see these mounds, which was natural when the enemy were cavalry. By and by they left the plain and went up and down the first mound; then as they were about to go up the second there were the barbarians volleying down the slope from the top javelins, slingstones, and arrows, and the masters could be seen flogging on the men! They wounded many, and defeated the Hellenic light-armed men, and shut them up in the square, so that slingers and bowmen were both quite useless among the mob all that day.

So the Hellenes had a hard time of it; but when they

[1] These were taken from the front or rear rank of the square, which had to be shortened.

tried to pursue they could scarcely get to the top in their
heavy arms, but the enemy quickly leaped away. When they
retired to the main army the same things happened; and on
the second mound the same again, so that they decided not
to move the soldiers from the third mound until they had
sent a party of light infantry from the right wing up the
mountains. As soon as these were posted above the pursuing enemy, the enemy no longer attacked the descending
troops for fear they should be cut off and find enemies on
both sides. So they proceeded for the rest of the day, the
army on the road moving over the foot-hills, the others
going parallel on the mountain-side, until they reached the
villages. They put eight surgeons in charge, for the wounded
were many.

They stayed there three days, partly for the sake of the
wounded, partly because there was plenty of food, wheatmeal, wine, barley collected for horses in great quantity.
These had been stored up for the regent of the country.

On the fourth day they came down into the plain. When
they came upon Tissaphernes with his forces, experience
taught them to encamp at the first village they saw and not
to march fighting all the while; for there were large numbers unable to fight, the wounded men and their bearers,
and those who carried the arms of the bearers. After they
had encamped, when the barbarians began to attack them
by their long shots, the Hellenes had much the best of it;
for there was a great difference between defending a fixt
position and making a running fight on the march.

When late afternoon came it was time for the enemy to
depart; for they never encamped at a less distance than
seven or eight miles, for fear that they might be attacked
in the night. The Persian army is good for nothing at night.
Their horses are tied up, and generally hobbled as well,
that they may not run away if cast loose; and if there
is any disturbance, the Persian has to saddle and bridle his

horse, and put on his corselet, and then mount—all difficult things at night when there is a disturbance too. That is why they used to encamp far away from the Hellenes. When our men noticed that they were about to go and the word went round, the trumpet sounded to pack up. The enemy heard it, and for some time they did not set out, but when it was late go they did, since they thought it did not pay to travel at night and come into camp. As soon as the Hellenes saw they were really off, they also broke up camp and marched, and did as much as seven miles. So the distance between the two armies was so great, that next day the enemy did not appear at all, nor the day after; but on the fourth day the barbarians had gone ahead by a night march and they seized a high position above the road by which the Hellenes had to go, a mountain spur on the right, under which was the descent into the plain.

When Cheirisophos noticed that the hill had been seized he called Xenophon from the rear, and ordered him to come up in front with the targeteers. But Xenophon did not bring them, for he saw Tissaphernes appear with his whole army. He rode up by himself and asked, "What is it?" The other said, "You can see; the hill above the descent has been seized, and we cannot pass unless we dislodge them. Why didn't you bring the targeteers?" He replied that he did not think it safe to leave the rear undefended when the enemy were in sight there. "Well, at least," said Cheirisophos, "it's high time to consider how we can drive the fellows from that hill." Then Xenophon looked up at the head of the hill above their army, and saw an approach from this to the peak where the enemy were, and he said, "The best thing for us, Cheirisophos, is to go for that height at once. If we seize it the men over the road can't hold their position. You stay with the army, if you wish, and I shall be glad to try that; or you go, and I'll stay." "Take your choice," said Cheirisophos, "you have my leave." Xenophon chose to

go. "I'm the younger," he said, but he asked for a detachment from the van, because it was a long way to bring men
from the rear. So Cheirisophos let him have the light infantry from the van, and took instead those from the centre.
He gave him also the 300 picked men that he had himself
in the van. They set off at full speed.

As soon as the enemy on the hill perceived their march
upon the height, they began to race for this same place.
Then there was a rare din, the Hellenic army cheering on
their men, and the army of Tissaphernes cheering theirs.
Xenophon rode by on his horse, shouting, "Men, remember
this is a race to Hellas! To your wives and children! One
little effort now, and we shall do the rest of our journey
without a blow!" Soteridas the Sicyonian shouted, "It isn't
fair, Xenophon! You ride on a horse, I'm tired out carrying
this shield!" Xenophon, hearing this, jumped off the horse,
and pushed the man out of his place, and took the shield
from him and went as fast as he could. He had his corselet
on, too, as it happened, so it was misery for him. "Look
sharp!" he called to the front, "Hurry up!" to the rear, and
he could hardly keep up himself. The other men whacked
Soteridas, and pelted him, and gave him plenty of hard
words, till they made him take back his shield and march
too. Xenophon mounted and rode on again, and led them
as long as the path allowed, but when it became too rough
he left the horse and made all haste on foot. So they got to
the place first, before the enemy.

v

Then the barbarians turned and fled where they could,
and the Hellenes occupied the height. The army of Tissaphernes and Ariaios turned away and went by another
road. Cheirisophos came down and encamped in a village
full of good things. There were many other villages full
of good things along the River Tigris. In the late afternoon

suddenly the enemy appeared on the plain, and they cut down some Hellenes who were scattered about the plain plundering; indeed, many herds of animals had been caught while trying to cross the river. There Tissaphernes' men began to burn the villages, and many of the Hellenes were downhearted for fear they might find no places to get provisions if the burning went on.

Cheirisophos had been to the rescue, and he was returning when Xenophon came riding down past the lines and called out as he met them, "There, men of Hellas! do you see they admit that the country is ours already? They have done what they made us promise not to do in their treaty! We were not to burn the king's country, and now they are burning it like a foreign country! Well, if they have provisions for themselves, they will see us going there too. Come, Cheirisophos," says he, "I think we ought to keep them from burning our country." Cheirisophos answered, "No, I don't; let's burn, too," says he, "and so they will stop sooner."

When they reached the camp most were busy about the provisions, but the captains and officers met. All was despondency now. On one side were high mountains, on one side a river so deep that even the spears could not sound it. In this unhappy state a Rhodian man came up and said, "I am ready, sirs, to take you across four thousand men at a time, if you provide me with what I want and pay me one talent." "What do you want?" they asked. "Skins I want," says he, "two thousand skins. I see plenty of sheep and goats and cattle and asses. Flay them and blow up the skins and they will easily give us a crossing. I will ask you too for the straps you put round the baggage animals. I fasten the skins together with these, I moor each one by tying stones to it and letting them down into the water like anchors, I carry them across by the current in a line and make fast the two ends, I throw wood on the top and earth over that. They will not sink, you will see that in a minute: every skin will hold up two men. They won't slip, the wood and earth will save them."

The captains thought this a pretty notion, but impossible to carry out, for there were numbers of cavalry on the other side to stop them; they would be down on the first lot and would not let them do anything at all. Then the next day they retreated again to the unburnt villages, after burning those they left; so the enemy did not ride after them, but watched them, and seemed to be wondering where they would turn now and what they meant to do. Then most were busy about the provisions, but the captains met again, and collecting their captives questioned them about the country round about, what each district was.

They said that the southern parts lay on the road towards Babylon and Media, by which indeed they had come; towards the east it led to Susa and Ecbatana, where the king is said to spend the summer; across the river to the west it led to Lydia, to Ionia; the road through the mountains and to the north led to the Kurds. These they said lived in the mountains and they were warlike; they did not obey the king; that once a royal army had invaded them, 112,000 strong, and not a man came back because of the difficulties of the country. But when there was truce between them and the governor in the plain, "we mix with them," says he, "and they mix with us."

After hearing this, the captains seated together those who claimed to know about each part, without revealing which way they meant to go. At last they decided that they were obliged to cross the mountains and get into the country of the Kurds. For the men said that when they had passed through this they would reach Armenia, a large and rich country which was the province of Orontas. Thence they said it would be easy to go wherever they wished. Upon this they offered sacrifice, so as to set out whenever it should seem to be the right time; for they feared that the pass over the mountains might have been occupied already. So they sent round the word that after dinner all should pack up and rest, and follow when the command was given.

BOOK FOUR

‏‏‎‎‎‏‏‎‎‎‏‏‎‎‎‏‏‎‎‎‏‏‎‎‎‏‏‎‎‎‏‏‎‎‎‏‏‎‎‎

I

It was about the last watch, and enough of the night was left for them to pass over the plain in darkness; then the word was sent round, and they rose up and marched, and by daylight they had reached the mountains. Cheirisophos was leading the army, with all the light-armed troops round him, and Xenophon with men-at-arms of the rear-guard followed without any light troops; for there seemed no danger that anyone would follow on the rear of an army going up. Cheirisophos reached the summit without seeing any of the enemy; then he led on, and each wave of the army as it rolled up followed into the villages which lie in the dells and corners of the hills. By this time all the Kurds had left their houses, with wives and children, and fled into the mountains; but plenty of provisions were to be had, and the houses were provided with huge numbers of brass pots. But the Hellenes took none of them, nor did they pursue the people. They spared them in the hope that the Kurds might let them pass through the country as friends, since they were enemies to the king; only they took all the provisions they found, for they had to do it. But the Kurds would not listen to any call, or do any other friendly act.

When the last of the Hellenes had come down from the summit into the villages, it was already dark; so narrow was the road that the ascent and descent had taken the whole day. Then some of the Kurds gathered and attacked the last lot, and killed some and wounded others with stones and arrows. They were only a few, for the Hellenic invasion had come as a surprise. But if there had been more, there was danger that a large part of the army would have been lost.

That night they spent in the open among the villages; but the Kurds lit numbers of fires on the mountains all round in sight of each other.

At dawn the captains and officers of the Hellenes met and decided to take with them only the strongest of their baggage-animals, and no more than were necessary; to leave all the rest, and to let go all captives lately taken that were in the army. Many animals and captives made the pace slow, and many of those in charge of them were out of the fight, and with all these men twice as much provision had to be found and carried. Heralds were sent round to cry these orders.

When breakfast was over they marched on; but the captains posted men beside the road at a narrow place: if they found any of the aforesaid things not left behind they took possession. The men mostly obeyed, but some did smuggle away a good-looking boy or woman.

They marched so far that day, sometimes fighting and sometimes resting; but next day came a heavy storm, yet they must go on for want of provisions. Cheirisophos led the way, Xenophon guarded the rear. The enemy attacked them vigorously, and in those narrow places they came close and shot arrows and slingstones, so the Hellenes were compelled to go slow what with chasing and coming back. Often Xenophon sent word for a halt, when the enemy attacked vigorously; sometimes Cheirisophos halted when the word came, but the last time he would not halt—he went on quickly and sent word to follow, so that it was clear something was up, but there was no time to go and see why he was in a hurry. So it became very much like a flight for the rearguard. There died a good man, Leonymos, a Laconian, shot with an arrow through shield and corselet into the ribs, and Basias, an Arcadian, right through the head.

As soon as they reached a halting-place, Xenophon went as he was straight to Cheirisophos, and reproached him: "Why didn't you halt? We were forced to fly and fight at the same time. And now two fine fellows are dead, and we could not take them up and bury them!" Cheirisophos answered, "Look at the mountains!" says he. "See! no way up anywhere: this one way you see steep too, and you can see all that mob. They have occupied the pass and they won't let us get out! That's why I made such a hurry and would not halt. I hoped to get there first and seize the pass, and the guides we have say there is no other way." Xenophon said, "Well, I have two captives. Those men were so troublesome that I laid ambush, which gave us a minute to breathe also; we killed a good few and took care to take some alive just in order to be guides, because they know the country."

Then he brought up the men, and questioned them separately, whether they knew any other road than the one they could see. One said no, although many terrors were applied; and since he had nothing useful to say, he was killed in sight of the other. The second said that the first said he knew no way because a daughter of his was married to a man over there; but he would take them by a road where even animals could go. Asked if there were any place ahead difficult to pass, he said there was a height which must be occupied first or nothing could get by.

Then it was decided to call the officers both of heavy and light infantry, to tell them all this and to ask if anyone were man enough to volunteer. From the heavy-armed two Arcadians came forward, Aristonymos, a Methydrian, and Agasias, a Stymphalian, while a third in rivalry, Callimachos, a Parrhasian, offered to lead volunteers from the whole army; "for I know," says he, "many young men will follow if I lead." Then they asked if any of the light-armed officers would join? Aristeas, a Chian, came forward, one who was often useful to the army for enterprises of this kind.

II

It was now late afternoon, and they ordered them to take a bite and go. They tied up the guide and handed him over to these; they arranged that if they could occupy the height, they were to guard it that night and sound the trumpet at dawn. Then the party on the height were to attack the enemy who held the pass, and they would themselves come out with succour as soon as they could.

With this arrangement the first party marched, about two thousand, in torrents of rain. Xenophon led his rearguard towards the visible pass, to draw the enemy's attention and to hide the others if possible as they moved round. The rearguard soon reached a ravine which they must traverse before they came to the steep part; and then the barbarians rolled down round stones of all sizes, some as big as a wagon-load, which hit the rocks and splintered in all directions like slingstones—it was absolutely impossible to go near the entrance. Some officers baulked in this place tried others, and this went on till it was dark; when they thought they could not be seen, they went away for supper, and some of the rearguard had not even had breakfast. But the enemy did not cease rolling the stones all night, as they could hear by the noise.

The party with the guide went round and caught the enemy outpost sitting round the fire; these they killed or chased away, and stayed there themselves, thinking they now held the height. But they did not hold it, for where the guards had been sitting there was a round hill above, along which ran the narrow path. However, there was an approach from this place to the enemy who were sitting on the visible road.

Thus they spent the night; and when daylight came they formed up and moved in silence towards the enemy. There was a mist, so they were able to come near without being seen. When they caught sight of each other, the trumpet sounded, and they rushed on the fellows cheering; the enemy did not stand, but left the road and fled; few were killed, for they went light. Cheirisophos and his men heard the trumpet, and charged straight up by the visible road; other captains pushed along by pathless ways wherever they happened to be, getting up as they could and hoisting each other by their spears. These were the first to meet the men who had occupied the height. Xenophon with half the rearguard marched by the road which the party with the guide had taken, for this was quite easy for baggage-animals; the other half he posted behind the animals. On the way they came to a hill above the road with enemy in possession, whom it was necessary either to cut down or else to be separated themselves from the other Hellenes. The men could have gone on above as the others had done, but the animals could not pass by any other way.

Here, shouting encouragement to each other, they charged straight up the front in company columns; they did not surround it but left a way for the enemy to escape if they wished. For a while the savages fought them off as well as they could, with arrows and spears, but they would not face them and ran away from the place. However, no sooner had they passed this hill than they saw another in front occupied, and determined to attack this again. But Xenophon saw that if he left the captured hill, the enemy might take it again and set on the baggage-train as it passed, and the train was long in that narrow path; so he left in charge captains Cephisodoros Cephisophon's son, an Athenian, and Amphicrates Amphidemos' son, an Athenian, and Archagoras, an exile from Argos, and himself marched with the others to the second hill and took it in the same way. After this a third hill remained, the steepest of them all, the one where that outpost had been taken in the night by the volunteers. But as soon as they came near, the savages left the hill without a blow, which astonished them all and made them suspect they had left it for fear of being encircled and besieged. But the truth was they saw from the height what was happening behind, and all moved upon the rearguard.

Now Xenophon with the youngest men climbed the hill, and told the others to go on, that the last companies might come up with them, until they could ground arms on the level beside the road. At this moment Archagoras arrived. He was in flight, and said that they had been dislodged from the first hill, and that Cephisodoros and Amphicrates were dead, with all the others who had not jumped down from the rocks and got back to the rearguard.

After this feat the natives came to a ridge opposite to the hill, and Xenophon spoke to them through an interpreter about a truce, and asked for the dead. They promised to give these back on condition that they would not burn the houses. Xenophon agreed to this. While they were parleying, and the rest of the army was passing, all the people of the place had been collecting; and as soon as they began to descend from the hill to join the others where they were halted, the enemy charged at once in great force with loud shouts, and when they were on the top of the hill which Xenophon had left, they rolled down rocks. One man's leg was broken, and Xenophon was deserted by the man who carried his shield; but Eurylochos of Lusia, one of the heavy-armed men, ran up to him and covered both with one shield, so they retreated, and the others joined the main body.

After this the whole Hellenic army united, and they encamped there in luxury; there were fine houses in plenty, and wine so plentiful that it was kept in cisterns of cement. Xenophon and Cheirisophos arranged to give up the guide in return for the dead bodies, and they rendered to the dead all the honours customary for brave men, so far as possible.

Next day they marched without guide; but the enemy hindered their passage by fighting and forestalling them at every narrow place. When they obstructed in front, Xenophon marched out from behind and made a loop over the mountains, and tried to get above them and break the barrier in front; when they attacked the rear, Cheirisophos marched out, and tried to get above the assailants and break the barrier behind. Thus they always looked after each other and each party supported the other. Sometimes when a party climbed a hill for this purpose the natives made it hot for them as they came down again, for they were so light that they could escape from quite close, as they had nothing but bows and slings. They were very good bowmen; they had bows of nearly three cubits, the arrows more than two cubits long. When they shot an arrow, they pressed the left foot upon the lower part of the bow as they drew the string; the arrows went through shield and corselet. When the Hellenes could get hold of any, they fitted thongs to them and used them as javelins. In these districts the Cretans were most useful; their commander was the Cretan Stratocles.

III

That night again they spent in the open, among the villages lying above the plain by the River Centritis,[1] width about two hundred feet, which was the frontier between Armenia and the country of the Kurds. There the Hellenes had time to breathe, delighted to see a plain. The river was distant from the mountains nearly a mile. There they had a happy night, with plenty to eat, talking and talking about the struggle now past. For they had spent seven days passing through the Kurds' country, fighting all the time, and they had suffered worse things than all the king and Tissaphernes did to them. They were quit of all that, they thought, and fell happily asleep.

At daybreak they saw horsemen somewhere across the river, armed and prepared to oppose a crossing, and footmen on the banks, marshalled above the horsemen, to hinder them from landing in Armenia. These were mercenaries of Orontas and Artuchas, Armenian and Mardian and Chaldæan. The Chaldæans were said to be free men and strong; they were armed with long wicker-work shields and lances. The banks where these ranks were standing were three or four furlongs away from the river; one road was in sight, leading upwards, apparently a regular highway. The Hellenes tried to cross by this road, but when they tried the water came over the breast, and the river-bed was rough with large slippery stones. They could not go through the water in arms, or else the river carried them off; they could not carry the arms on their heads, or they were bare against arrows and other missiles. So they retreated, and encamped by the riverside. And where they had spent the last night themselves on the mountain, they saw the Kurds assembled, armed, in large numbers.

Then the Hellenes were very despondent when they saw how difficult it was to cross the river, and when they saw

[1] E. Tigris

troops ready to resist, when they saw the Kurds behind ready to fall on them while they crossed.

So they stayed there in great despondency that day and night. But Xenophon saw a dream. He thought he was fastened in irons, and the fetters dropt off of themselves, so that he was free, and able to straddle as wide as he liked. In the early morning he went and told Cheirisophos that he had hopes all would be well, and described his dream. Cheirisophos was glad, and as soon as the light of dawn came the captains made sacrifice, all being present; and the omens were favourable even in the very first victim. Leaving the sacrifice, the captains and officers sent round word for the army to breakfast.

While Xenophon sat at breakfast, two young men ran up; for all knew that anyone might come to him, at breakfast or supper, or if he slept, could awake him, and tell anything he had to propose for the war. They told him, then, that they had been gathering firewood, and they saw opposite, among some rocks which came down to the river, an old man with a woman and girls laying something like bags of clothes in a cave in the rock. As they watched they thought it was a safe place to cross; at least enemy horsemen could not come near that place. So they stript and went in naked holding their knives, expecting to swim for it; but they simply marched on and crossed and never wetted their middle; then they took the clothes and came back.

So Xenophon poured a libation at once, and told the young men to fill up, and to pray the gods who had shown the dream and the ford that they might accomplish what remained with good success. After this, he took the young men straight to Cheirisophos, and they told their story. Cheirisophos listened, and poured a libation himself. Afterwards they sent round word to pack up; then called a meeting of the captains, and discussed how they could best cross and conquer those in front and not be hurt by those behind. They decided that Cheirisophos was to lead across with half the army, and the other half was to stay with Xenophon, and the baggage-train to cross in the middle.

When all was arranged they marched; the young men guided them, with the river on the left. It was about half a mile to the ford, and as they marched the troops of horse opposite kept pace with them.

When they reached the ford and the riverbanks, they grounded arms; and first Cheirisophos himself put a wreath on his head and threw off his cloak, and took up his arms, giving command to the others to do the same; and he ordered the subalterns to lead their companions in column, part on his left and part on his right. Meanwhile the soothsayers were sacrificing over the river; the enemy were shooting with bows and slings, but they were out of range. When the omens were favourable, all the men chanted the battle-hymn and cheered, and the women all raised the woman's hosanna of triumph, for there were many women in the camp.

Cheirisophos then plunged in with his division; but Xenophon took the handiest men of the rearguard, and doubled back to the passage on the road which led away into the Armenian mountains, pretending that he wished to cross there and cut off the horsemen along the river. The enemy saw Cheirisophos and his forces easily crossing the water, and Xenophon doubling back, and then fearing they might be cut off they galloped away towards the upper crossing, but as soon as they reached the road they turned upwards towards the mountains. Then Lycios, who commanded the division of horsemen in the army of Cheirisophos, and Aischines, who commanded the light-armed troops, followed the cavalry when they saw them galloping away; and the soldiers called out, "Don't let them get away! Follow into the mountains!" However, Cheirisophos did not pursue the cavalry when his crossing was made, but

climbed the high banks opposite the place to attack the
enemy there above. But these saw their own cavalry in
flight, and saw the men-at-arms moving to attack them, and
left the higher ground above the river.

Now Xenophon saw that all went well across the river
and he doubled back towards the crossing troops; for the
Kurds were visible coming down from the hills to attack
the last men.

Cheirisophos already held the upper parts, and Lycios
with his little troop in pursuit caught the last of their baggage-train, and with them a load of fine dress and drinking-
cups. The last of the Hellenic baggage-train and followers
had just crossed, when Xenophon returned and took a stand
opposite the Kurds. He ordered the captains to form up
their companies in squads, and to deploy to the left in line
of squads, the captains and subalterns facing the Kurds with
sergeants in the rear facing the river.

When the Kurds saw the rearguard bare of the camp-
followers and looking just a handful of men, they advanced
more quickly singing songs of their own. But Cheirisophos,
being now in safety, sent back the light-armed troops and
the bowmen and slingers to Xenophon, and told them to
obey his orders. Xenophon saw them ready to cross; he sent
a messenger with orders to stay near the river but not to go
in; but when he began to cross himself, they should enter
the river to meet him, on the left and right, as if to cross,
with javelins on the thong and arrows on the string, but
they were not to go far into the river. To his own men the
orders were, "As soon as a slingstone hits a shield and you
hear the rattle, chant the battle-hymn, and at the enemy;
when the enemy turn and the trumpet sounds the attack,
right about face and the sergeants lead, all double and each
cross opposite his post so as not to interfere with each other:
first man over is best man!"

The Kurds saw only a handful of men left, for many of

those who had been ordered to wait were gone to look after their animals or baggage or women: at once they attacked boldly and began to sling and shoot. The Hellenes chanted their battle-hymn and charged at the double, but the enemy did not wait; for they were well equipt for running up and running off in the mountains, but not for a fight hand to hand. Then the trumpet sounded the charge; the enemy ran faster than ever, the Hellenes turned about and made for the river at full speed. Some of the enemy noticed this and ran back to the river, and wounded a few with arrows, but most of them could still be seen in full flight even when the Hellenes were across. The others who came to meet them went too far in their ardour, and had to cross again behind Xenophon; some of these also were wounded.

IV

When they had crossed they formed up together about midday and marched through Armenia, all plain and smooth little hills, not less than five leagues; for there were no villages near the river, because of their wars with the Kurds. But the village they reached was large and had a palace for the governor, and towers over most of the houses; provisions in abundance. From there they marched two stages, 10 leagues, until they reached the source of the Tigris River. From there they marched three stages, 15 leagues, to the River Teleboas; a fine river, but not large, and there were many villages about the river. This district was called Southern Armenia; the lieutenant-governor was Tiribazos, the King's Friend, and his was the right to mount the king on horseback when he was present. This man rode up with a troop of horse, and sent forward an interpreter to say he wished to parley with the commanders. The captains decided to hear him, and coming within hearing they asked what he wished. He replied that he wished for a truce, on these terms: he would not damage the Hellenes and they should not burn the houses, but take what provisions they needed. The captains agreed, and truce was made on those terms.

Thence they marched three stages over the plain, 15 leagues, and Tiribazos followed with his force about a mile behind. Then they reached the palace, and many villages round, full of all sorts of provisions. While they were encamping came a heavy fall of snow; and in the morning it was decided to billet the companies with their captains among the villages, for they saw no enemy, and it seemed to be safe with all that snow. There they had all the good things they wanted, sacrificial victims, corn, fragrant old wines, raisins, all kinds of vegetables.

But some stragglers from the camp reported that they had seen large numbers of fires in the night. So billeting seemed no longer safe; they must assemble the army again, and so they did. The sky seemed likely to clear then, but while they slept there came snow without end which covered the arms and the men lying there. The snow was a great hindrance to the animals, and nobody wanted to get up, for it kept them snug and warm where they lay unless it slipt off. At last Xenophon condescended to stand up in his shirt and split wood, and then one or another got up and pulled the log out of his hands and began to split, then others got up and lit fires and oiled themselves; there was plenty of oil there, hog's lard and oil from sesame and bitter almonds and turpentine, which they used instead of olive oil. A balsam also was made from the same.

After this they decided to billet again under shelter. The men with loud shouts of delight rushed back to the shelter and provisions; and then any who had burnt the houses they left just out of mischief were sorry for it when they had bad quarters. The next night they sent Democrates of Tenos with a few men to the mountains where stragglers said they had seen the fires; for this man had been found before to bring truthful reports; and when he said it was so, it was, and when he said it wasn't, it was not. When he came back he said he had seen no fires, but he brought back a prisoner armed with Persian bow and quiver, and a bill such as the Amazons carry. Questioned, he said he was a Persian, and that he was foraging for provisions from the army of Tiribazos. They asked how large was the army, and why it had been formed. He replied that Tiribazos had his own force and some mercenaries, Chalybians and Taochians; said he was prepared to fall on the Hellenes while they crossed the mountains, in narrow places with only one road. The captains decided on hearing this to assemble the army; they marched at once with the man as guide, leaving guards under the command of Sophainetos, a Stymphalian.

While they were crossing, the light-armed troops going on before caught sight of the enemy camp, and without waiting for the heavy troops rushed on the camp with loud shouts. The natives, hearing the noise, did not stay, they ran for it; but still some were killed, and horses were taken, about twenty, and the tent of Tiribazos was taken, and in it couches with silver feet, and cups, and men who said they were bakers and butlers. When the captains of the heavy-armed heard this report, they decided to return to their camp as quickly as they could to prevent an assault on those left behind. They sounded the recall and retired, and reached the camp the same day.

v

Next day they decided to march as quickly as possible, before the enemy could collect and occupy the narrows. They packed up and marched at once, through deep snow, having several guides; and the same day they got over the height where Tiribazos meant to attack them, and encamped there. From that place they marched three desert stages, 15 leagues, and reached the River Euphrates, which they crossed

waist-deep. The source was said to be not far away. From
there they marched through deep snow over a plain, three
stages, 15 leagues. The third was difficult, and a north wind
blew in their faces, parching everything everywhere and
freezing the men. There one of the seers advised them to
sacrifice to the wind, and sacrifice they did. The answer to
their prayers was manifest at once to all, when the violence
of the wind abated. But the snow was a fathom deep, so
that many animals and slaves were lost, and soldiers too,
about thirty. They kept fire burning all night, and so got
through; there was plenty of wood in that stage, but those
who came up late found none. Those who had been there
long and lit the fire would not let the late ones come near
the fire unless they gave them some of their wheat or anything else they had eatable. Here, then, they all shared together what they had. Where the fire burned great holes
were made in the snow right down to the soil, and so it was
possible to measure the depth of the snow.

The whole of the next day they were marching through
snow, and many men were faint with hunger. Xenophon
was in the rearguard, and he did not know what was the
matter with them. Some one who knew about it told him it
was hunger faintness, and they would get up if he gave them
something to eat; so he went round the baggage animals,
and if he found food anywhere he gave it round, or sent
those who could run about to give some to the sufferers. As
soon as they had had a bite, up they got and marched on.

They marched until when darkness came Cheirisophos
reached a village, and found women and girls fetching
water from the fountain in front of their wall. These women
asked who they were. The interpreter answered in Persian
that they came from the king to the governor. They said
he was not there, but about one league away. Since it was
late, they went together with the women to the village
headman inside the stockade. Then Cheirisophos and all

who could encamped there, but the rest of the army, those who could not finish the march, spent the night foodless and fireless; some of the men perished there. Parties of the enemy were always following, and carried off disabled animals and fought over them together. Men also were left behind who had been blinded by the snow or lost their toes by frostbite. It did some good to the eyes if the men marched holding something black before their eyes; for the feet, to keep them moving without rest all the time and to take off the shoes at night. But if any slept with shoes on, the straps worked into the feet and the shoes froze; for the old shoes were gone, and they had to make them of raw leather from untanned hides newly flayed.

Through such necessities some of the soldiers were left behind, and when they saw a black patch where the snow had disappeared, they imagined that it had thawed there, and indeed it had thawed, because of a hot spring which was steaming in a dingle close by. There these men turned aside and sat, and said they would not go on. Xenophon with some of his rearguard noticed this, and begged them with prayers and entreaties not to stay behind, telling them that packs of the enemy were on the chase. At last he grew angry, but they told him to cut their throats, march they could not. Then it seemed best to frighten the enemy following, if he could, and keep them off the weary men. It was dark now, and the enemy were following in confusion and quarrelling over what they had. Then the rearguard, who were well and strong enough, jumped up and ran for the enemy, and the weary men shouted as loud as they could and banged spears against their shields. The enemy were frightened, and smashed through the snow into the dingle, and not a sound was heard from them again.

Xenophon and his party told the weary men that someone would come for them to-morrow, and marched on. They

had not gone half a mile when they came on their soldiers
on the road, lying upon the snow wrapt up and trying to
sleep, without any guard at all; and he made them get up.
They said those in front would not go on. He passed by,
and sent on the strongest of his light troops to see what was
in the way. They reported that the whole army was sleeping
like that. Then Xenophon settled down there for the night,
without fire or food, after posting such guards as he could.

When day was near Xenophon sent the youngest of his
men back to the weary men, with orders to make them get
up and force them to march. Meanwhile Cheirisophos sent
men from the village to see how the rear was doing. Glad
indeed they were to see them, and handed over the weary
men to be taken to the camp, while they marched themselves, and two or three miles farther on they reached the
village where Cheirisophos had spent the night. When they
met, they thought it was safe to billet the companies in the
villages. Cheirisophos remained where he was, and the
others drew lots for the villages in sight, and each led his
men to their place.

Now Polycrates, an Athenian officer, asked for special
leave, and taking the most active of his men, he ran to the
village allotted to Xenophon, and found all the villagers inside, and their headman, and colts which were being reared
for the king's tribute, seventeen, and the headman's daughter nine days wedded; her husband was out hunting hares,
and he was not caught in the village. The houses were under
ground, the mouth like a well, roomy underneath; the people went down by ladders, but the animals had a way dug
for them. In the houses were sheep, goats, cattle, birds, and
their young; all the beasts were fed indoors on green stuff.
There was also wheat and barley and vegetables, and barley-
wine in tubs; there were barley-grains floating on the wine
at the rim, and straws lay there, large and small, without

knots. If you were thirsty, you picked up one of these and sucked through it. It was very strong wine if drunk neat, and the taste was delicious when you were used to it.

Xenophon made the headman of this village share his table, and told him to fear nothing; they would not rob him of his children, but they would fill the house with provisions before they went, if he would do good service to the army and guide them to some other tribe. The man promised, and with all goodwill showed him where the wine was buried.

That night, billeted thus, all the soldiers rested in the midst of abundance, keeping the headman under guard and his family with him safe in sight. On the next day Xenophon took the headman before Cheirisophos. Whenever he passed a village he looked in and found them everywhere feasting and making merry. The people never let them go without offering breakfast; everywhere on the same table were piles of lamb, kid, pork, veal, fowl, with all sorts of cakes, both wheaten and barley. When one would show goodwill by drinking your health, he dragged you to the bowl, and you must duck your head and gulp it up like a bullock. They let the headman take away whatever he liked. But he would accept nothing, only if he saw any of his own kinsmen, he took him away with him.

When they reached Cheirisophos, they found them there in their quarters, garlanded with hay and served by Armenian boys in their native costume; they made signs to the boys as if they were deaf and dumb to show what they wanted. After Cheirisophos and Xenophon had greeted one another affectionately, they asked the headman together through the interpreter who spoke Persian, "What country is this?" He said, "Armenia." They asked again for whom he was breeding the colts. He said, "Tribute for the king." The neighbouring country, he said, was the Chalybeans,

and pointed where the road was. Then Xenophon led him
to his own servants, and gave him an oldish horse which he
had caught to feed up and sacrifice, because he heard that
the horse was sacred to the Sun [1]: he was afraid it might
die, for it had suffered from the march. He took one of the
colts himself, and gave a colt each to the other captains and
officers. The horses in this place were smaller than the Persian, but much more spirited. Then the headman taught him
to wrap bags round the feet of the baggage-horses when
they are driven through snow; without the bags they sink
down to the belly.

VI

When the eighth day came, he gave the headman as guide
to Cheirisophos, but left all the headman's household except
his son, just growing up; this boy he entrusted to Pleisthenes
of Amphipolis, and he should be given back if the man was
a good guide. They filled his house with all the supplies
they could find and marched away. The headman guided
them through the snow; the third stage came, and still there
were no villages, which made Cheirisophos very angry. The
man said there were no villages in that part. Cheirisophos
then struck him, but he did not bind him, and in consequence that night he deserted, and left his son. This was the
only difference between Xenophon and Cheirisophos in the
whole march, the violence done to the guide and the care-
lessness. Pleisthenes fell in love with the boy, and brought
him home, and found him most faithful.

After this they marched seven stages at 5 leagues a day to
the River Phasis, width 100 feet. Thence they marched two
stages, 10 leagues, and in the descent they were met by
Chalybeans and Taothans and Phasians. When Cheirisophos caught sight of the enemy at the pass, he halted
about three miles away, that he might not approach the en-

[1] This was an Indian custom; a horse was consecrated and let loose.

emy marching in column. He sent order round to form line
of companies in column. When the rearguard came up he
summoned captains and officers, and said:

"The enemy, as it appears, hold the pass, and we must
consider how best to fight. I think it best to order the men
to breakfast, and then we should deliberate whether to cross
to-day or to-morrow."

"My opinion," said Cleanor, "is that when we have
breakfasted, we should arm at once and attack. If we delay
to-day, the present enemy will be bolder, and it is likely
that many others will join them while they are confident."

Now Xenophon spoke. "My opinion is this. If a fight
cannot be avoided, we ought to be ready to fight our
strongest. But if we wish to traverse the pass most easily, we
should consider how to pass with fewest wounds and
smallest loss of men. What we see of the mountain is seven
or eight miles across, and the men waiting for us are visible
only on the road; it is much better, then, to try to steal some
part of the empty space and get round unseen, if we can,
than to attack fortifications and men prepared to fight. For
it is much easier to climb a steep place without fighting
and then to go along the flat with enemies on each side;
without fighting we can see better at night what is in front
of our feet than we can by day while fighting; and the rough
way before our feet will be easier to tread without fighting
than the level path when our heads are being battered. To
steal a march does not seem impossible to me, since we can
go by night so as not to be seen, and keep far enough away
so as not to be heard; and if we make a feint of attacking
here the mountain will be more deserted, since the enemy
would remain all together where they are.

"But why do I give my notions about stealing? You
Lacedaimonians, as I hear, Cheirisophos, you who belong to
the Spartan peers, practise the art of stealing from boyhood;
it is not base to steal, but honourable, where the law does

not forbid. But to steal cleverly and not to be caught, that is lawful surely, I think, and to be thrashed if you are caught stealing. Then now's the time to show off your education, and take care not to be caught stealing a bit of the hill and not to be thrashed."

"Well indeed," said Cheirisophos, "I hear you Athenians are clever at stealing public funds, although there is terrible risk for the thief, and your biggest men are the biggest thieves, if the biggest men are honoured with high office! Then just show off your own education!" "All right," said Xenophon, "I'm ready! After supper I'll take the rearguard and go and capture the mountain. I have my guides; for the light-armed among my attendant thieves have caught some by lying in wait. I hear from them that the mountain is not impassable, but goats and cattle feed there; so if we can once get a bit of mountain, our baggage-animals can go too. And I expect the enemy won't stay here themselves, when they see us on the heights like them; even now they will not come down to meet us on equal terms."

Cheirisophos said, "And why should you go and leave your rearguard? Just tell others to go, if no good volunteers turn up." Then Aristonymos the Methydrian came with men-at-arms, and Aristeas the Chian with light troops, and Nicomachos the Oitaian with light troops, and they arranged to kindle plenty of fires when they held the heights.

With this arrangement they took breakfast; and after that Cheirisophos led the army about a mile towards the enemy, to make them believe that the attack would come there.

After supper, when night came, the men told off went and got possession of the mountain, and the others rested where they were. When the enemy had news that the mountain was held, they awoke and lit many fires through the night. At daybreak Cheirisophos sacrificed and led along the road, those who held the mountain advanced along the heights, and most of the enemy remained at the pass, but a detachment went to meet those on the mountain. Before the main bodies came together, the two parties on the heights met, the Hellenes conquered and gave chase. Meanwhile on the plain the light-armed Hellenes went at the double towards the ranks of the enemy, and Cheirisophos followed with the heavy troops at quick march. The enemy on the road took to flight as soon as they saw the others worsted on the hills. Not many of them were killed, but they left large quantities of wicker shields, which the Hellenes chopt up with their swords and made useless. When all had come up they sacrificed and set up a trophy, and then descended into the plain, where they found villages full of good things.

VII

After this they marched into the Taochian country, five stages, 30 leagues. Provisions now failed them; for the Taochians lived in strong places, where they had carried up all their stores. The army reached a strong place, not a city, a place without houses, but men and women had all gathered there with many flocks and herds. Cheirisophos, however, attacked at once; one battalion attacked, and failed, then another and another again, for they could not surround it in full force, because the sides were too steep all round. When Xenophon arrived with the rearguard, both light and heavy troops, Cheirisophos said:

"Just in the nick of time. This place must be taken; the army has no food if we don't take the place."

They consulted. "Why don't you walk in?" asked Xenophon. Cheirisophos answered, "There's the way in, as you see, the only one; whenever we try to walk in, they roll down stones from that projecting rock. If anyone's caught, see what happens," and he pointed to men with legs and ribs broken to pieces. "If they use up all their stones," Xenophon said, "you may just walk in—nothing in the way, I think? All I can see is a few men, and only two or three armed. And the distance to go, as you see yourself, is hardly fifty yards to cross exposed, and there are thick groves of pines at intervals; if men were to shelter behind them, what harm would they get either from rolling stones or thrown stones? The rest is only a few yards, which they must run when the shower of stones is a bit slack." "Oh yes," said Cheirisophos. "But as soon as we begin to approach the grove, down come the showers of stones!" "Just what we want," said he, "they will use up their stones quicker. Let us choose a place where only a little space will be left to run, if we can run, and it will be easier to get back if we wish."

Then Cheirisophos went on and Xenophon, with Callimachos the Parrhasian, a subaltern, the officer in command of the rearguard officers on that day; the other officers remained in a safe place. After this a number of men came out under the trees, about seventy, not all together but one by one, each guarding himself as he could. Others were standing by outside the trees, Agasias the Stymphalian and Aristonymos the Methydrian, also officers of the rearguard, and others; for there was not safe standing under the trees for more than the one company.

Then Callimachos had a happy thought. He went two or three steps beyond his tree, and when the stones began to fly, he got back easily; but at each advance more than ten cartloads of stones were wasted. When Agasias saw Callimachos doing this and the whole army looking on, he was afraid he might not be first man in; so he called none of those near, neither Aristonymos nor Eurylochos the Lusian, his comrades, nor anyone else, but he's off by himself and runs past the others. Callimachos saw him rushing by and caught the rim of his shield: meanwhile Aristonymos ran past them both, and after him Eurylochos, for all these were rivals in daring, each trying to beat the other all the time: and when they had all raced in, not one stone came from above.

Then there was an awful sight. The women threw down their children and themselves upon them, and the men the same. One Aineias, a Stymphalian officer, saw a man in a fine costume running to throw himself over, and caught hold of him to prevent it, but the man dragged him down too, and both went rolling over the rocks and perished. Few human beings were left alive, but numbers of cattle and asses and sheep.

From that place they marched through the Chalybean country, seven stages, 50 leagues. These were the stoutest men they had met, and ready for hand-to-hand fighting. They wore corselets of linen reaching to the groin, and instead of the side-wings thick bunches of cords; they had greaves also and head-pieces, and by the belt a knife like the Laconian dagger, which they used to butcher any they caught and cut off their heads, which they carried away, and they sang and danced when the enemy were likely to see them. They had also a spear some five cubits long with a single spike. These kept in their towns, and when the Hellenes passed, they always followed fighting. They had houses in their strongholds, and their stores of provisions were there, so the Hellenes got nothing from that part, but they lived on the livestock which they had taken from the Taochians.

After this the Hellenes reached the Harpasos River, width 400 feet. From there they marched through the Scythenians, four stages, 20 leagues, over a plain to some villages, in which they stayed three days and got supplies. From these they passed on four stages, 20 leagues, to an inhabited city, large and prosperous, which was called Gymnias.

Here the governor of the place sent the Hellenes a guide to lead them through a country which was hostile to himself. This man, when he came, told them that in five days he would take them to a place where they could have sight of the sea; they might kill him if he didn't. As soon as he passed the boundaries he advised them to burn and destroy the country; so it was clear that that was why he came, not friendliness to the Hellenes.

They reached the mountain in the fifth day; its name was Theches.[1] When the first men reached the summit and caught sight of the sea there was loud shouting. Xenophon and the rearguard, hearing this, thought that more enemies were attacking in front; for some were following behind them from the burning countryside, and their own rearguards had killed a few men and captured others, and taken wicker shields, covered with raw hairy oxhides, about twenty. But when the shouts grew louder and nearer, as each group came up it went pelting along to the shouting men in front, and the shouting was louder and louder as the crowds increased. Xenophon thought it must be something very important; he mounted his horse, and took Lycios with his horsemen, and galloped to bring help. Soon they heard the soldiers shouting "Sea! sea!" and passing the word along.

Then the rearguard also broke into a run, and the horses and baggage animals galloped too. When they all reached the summit then they embraced each other, captains and officers and all, with tears running down their cheeks. And suddenly—whoever sent the word round—the soldiers brought stones and made a huge pile. Upon it they threw heaps of raw hides and sticks and the captured shields, and the guide cut them up with his own hands and told them to do the same.

After this the Hellenes let the guide go; they presented

[1] Gymnias is identified with Erzeroum, but not certainly; and Theches perhaps Baïlburt (Ainsworth, p. 188).

him publicly with a horse and a silver bowl and Persian
dress and ten darics; he asked especially for their rings, and
the soldiers gave him great numbers of them. He pointed
out a village where they could encamp, and the road to the
Macronian country, and in the evening he departed to
travel through the night.

VIII

From that place the Hellenes marched through the Macronians, three stages, 10 leagues. On the first day they
reached a river which was the boundary between Macronians and Scythenians. They had on the right above them
very difficult country, and on the left another river into
which the frontier river runs, and this they must cross.
This was lined with trees of no great size but thickly
packed. The Hellenes cut them down as they went, eager
to get out of the place as soon as possible. But the Macronians came armed with wicker shields and spears, and
wearing hairy tunics, and stood in order opposite the ford
to oppose them, and threw stones into the river, but they
were out of range and did no harm.

Then one of the light-armed men came to Xenophon. He
said he had been a slave in Athens, and knew the language
of these people. "And I think," he says, "this is my own
country; and if there is no objection, I will go and parley
with them." "No objection at all," said he. "Parley away,
and find out first who they are." The man asked, and they
said Macronians. "Ask them," said Xenophon, "why they
are mustered here and wish to be enemies to us." They answered, "Because you are invading our country." The captains told him to say that they would do no damage. "We
have been at war with the king, and we are on the way to
Hellas and want to get to the sea." The natives asked if
pledges would be given for this. They answered they wished
for a treaty between them. Then the natives gave them a

native spear, and the Hellenes gave the natives a Hellenic spear, for these were their pledges, as they said; both parties called the gods to witness.

After this the Macronians helped to fell trees and to make a road; they would allow them to pass, and they mingled with the Hellenes, and provided a market such as they could, and in three days brought them to the boundary of the Colchians, and left them there. In this place was a high mountain, but passable, and upon the mountain the Colchians were mustered. First the Hellenes formed in battle array to attack the mountain; then the captains met to consider how best to attack. Now Xenophon said, "We should not fight in line but form in company columns, because the line will break at once, as the mountain will be easy here and difficult there; it will dishearten the men as soon as they see their line broken up. Then if we make a front several men deep the enemy will overlap us, and have men to spare to be used where they like; or if the line is only two or three deep, we must not be surprised if they cut it with thick volleys of missiles and massed attacks. If the line is cut in one place, that will be dangerous for the whole. My opinion is, that we form in company columns, leaving the columns so far apart that the extreme columns overlap the enemy wings; thus we shall overlap the whole enemy line, and by leading in column the strongest will go on first, and where the way is easy, each of the other columns may follow in turn. It will not be easy for the enemy to penetrate the spaces between the columns, and it will not be easy to cut up a company standing in column. If one of the columns is hard pressed the nearest shall help. And if one of the columns can get to the top, not a man of the enemy will stand."

This was agreed, and they formed in line of company columns. Then Xenophon passed from right to left, addressing the soldiers: "Men, these whom you see alone are left in the way, to keep us from reaching at once the place we have been seeking so long. These men, if we can, we must devour raw!"

When they had formed the companies in column and all were in place, there were about eighty companies of heavy-armed troops, each company about one hundred men. The light-armed and the bowmen they divided into three parts, one outside the left wing, one outside the right wing, and one in the centre, each about six hundred strong. Then the word went round to offer their prayers; they prayed aloud, and chanted the battle-hymn, and advanced. Cheirisophos and Xenophon and their parties of light troops advanced outside the enemy line on the left and right; when the enemy saw them, they also ran to left and right trying to keep parallel with them, and broke apart so that there was a large empty space in the centre. The light troops of the Arcadian regiment, commanded by Aischines the Arcadian, thought the enemy were in flight and pursued with loud cries; the Arcadian heavies went with them, commanded by Cleanor the Orchomenian.

And when the enemy began to run they could stand no longer, and it really turned to a flight pell-mell. The Hellenes marched up the mountains and encamped in a number of villages with plenty of provisions. They found nothing remarkable there except the great numbers of beehives; all those who ate the honey went out of their senses, and vomited and purged, and not a man of them could stand straight on his feet. If they ate only a little they seemed like drunken men, if they ate much, like madmen; some even died of it. So they lay in heaps as if there had been a rout, and they were very unhappy about it. Next day no-one died, but about the same time of day they came back to their senses; in another day or two they got up dazed as if they had been drugged.

From that place they marched two stages, 7 leagues, and

reached the sea at Trapezûs,[1] a Hellenic inhabited city on the Euxine, a colony of Sinope, lying in the Colchian country. There they stayed about thirty days in the Colchian villages, and from these they despoiled the Colchian country. The Trapezuntians provided market, and welcomed their fellow-countrymen and presented them with their gifts of hospitality, cattle and wheaten flour and wine. They made arrangements with them about the neighbouring Colchians, particularly those who lived in the plain, and gifts of cattle came from them also. After this they prepared the sacrifice which they had vowed; they had cattle enough to sacrifice fully to Zeus Saviour and Heracles and the other gods, all they had vowed.

They held also a contest of games and sports on the hill where they were encamped. To find a racecourse and superintend the games they chose one Dracontios, a Spartan noble who had been banished as a boy for striking a boy with his knife and killing him by accident.

After the sacrifice they gave over the hides to Dracontios, and told him to take them to his ground. He pointed to the hill where they stood, and says he, "This hill is the best possible place to race wherever you like." "Oh," said they, "and how can they wrestle on this hard bushy ground?" He said, "So much the worse for the man who gets a fall." There was the two hundred yards for boys, mostly captives; in the long race [2] the Cretans ran, more than sixty of them; others did wrestling and boxing and both combined,[3] and it was a fine sight; there were plenty of entries, and plenty of rivalry with all their comrades looking on. There was horse-racing too; they had to ride down the precipice into the sea, and back again to the altar. On the way down most of them rolled along; on the way up the horses could hardly walk up that sheer steep. What shouts, what roars of laughter, what cheers!

[1] Trebizond
[2] twenty stades, between two and three miles
[3] the pancration

uuu

I

After this, they met and deliberated about the rest of their travels.

First Leon, a Thurian, rose, and spoke as follows:

"To speak for myself, sirs, I'm tired out by this time, with packing up and marching and doubling and carrying arms and falling in and keeping guard and fighting. I want a little rest now from these hardships. We have the sea, then let's go by sea the rest of the way, lying flat like Odysseus, till we get to Hellas."

There was great cheering at this, "Good! good!" and someone else said the same, and so said all of them. Then Cheirisophos rose, and said:

"I have a friend, sirs, Anaxibios, who is now Lord High Admiral at home, as it happens. If you will send me there, I think I shall bring you back ships of war and transports to carry you. If you want to go by sea, wait until I return; I won't be long."

On hearing this, the men were delighted and voted that he should sail, the sooner the better.

Next Xenophon rose and spoke:

"So Cheirisophos is despatched for ships, and we are to wait for him. But what is the proper thing to do while we wait? I will tell you.

"First, we must get provisions from enemy country. Our market is not enough, and we have nothing to buy with, except some few. But this country is enemy country, so there is danger of losing many lives if you march for provisions carelessly and unguardedly. I propose that you go in regular parties to get provisions, and so keep safe, and not go wandering about anyhow; and that we should arrange this for you." Agreed. "Another thing now: listen. Some of you will go for spoil. I think it is best, therefore, that anyone about to go for spoil shall inform us, and tell us where he is going. We wish to know how many go and how many stay; we wish to help in preparing, if necessary, and if any need succour, we want to know where the succour is needed; if some unpractised hands undertake anything, we would offer advice, and try to discover the strength of those he would attack." Agreed also. "Something more," said he. "Don't forget that the enemy have plenty of time to make raids too, and they have a right to attack us because we hold what is theirs; they are planted up there above us. I propose, therefore, that guards be set round the camp; if we take it in turns to watch and to spy, the enemy would be less able to hunt us. Then again, look here: if we knew for certain that Cheirisophos would bring us transports enough, there would be no need for what I'm going to say; but this is uncertain, in fact, so I propose that we try to collect vessels from hereabouts. Then if he does bring them, and we also have some here, there will be all the more to carry us; but if not, we will use what we have. I often see vessels sailing past, let us ask the Trapezuntians for the loan of warships, and bring the vessels in and take off the rudders and keep them until we have enough to hold us. In that way perhaps we shall not lack the transport we need." This was agreed to. "Consider then," he said, "whether it is fair that we find food by a general subscription for the crews we shall bring in, as long as they wait our pleasure here; and we should agree on the passage-money, that we may repay service with service." Agreed also. "And in case it turns out that we cannot succeed in collecting vessels enough, I propose that the cities along the sea-coast be instructed to put the roads in good repair, for I hear they are in a bad state. They will obey, because they fear us and will be glad to get rid of us."

Then there were loud outcries, "No, not by road, we won't go by road!" When Xenophon saw their folly, he did not put this to the vote, but he privately persuaded the cities easily to repair the road, by telling them that they would get out of the way more quickly if the roads were in good repair. They also got a fifty-oar galley from Trapezûs, and put in command Dexippos, a farmer from Laconia. But he neglected his duty of collecting vessels, and sailed clean away right out of the Euxine, ship and all. Later he had his deserts; for in Thrace he tried to meddle in the affairs of Seuthes,[1] and he was killed by Nicandros the Laconian. They got also a thirty-oar galley, and put an Athenian Polycrates in command; he brought in all the vessels he took to the camp. Any freights they took out of the vessels, and set guards to keep them safe, and kept the vessels for the transport.

While these things were being done, the Hellenes went out marauding, and some succeeded but some did not. Cleainetos led his company and another to a dangerous place, where he was killed and many with him.

II

By and by they could no longer find provisions within a day's raid. Then Xenophon procured guides from Trapezûs,

[1] an Odrysian prince

and led half the army against the Drilai, leaving half to
guard the camp; for the Colchians, having been ejected
from their houses, were in large masses on the hills above.
The Trapezuntians would not guide them to places where
it was easy to find provisions, because the natives were
friendly to them; but they were ready enough to guide them
against the Drilai, who had done them much damage.
These were mountainous places and hard to approach, and
the people were the most warlike of all on the Euxine.

When the Hellenes reached the highlands, the Drilai
burnt all the villages which they thought might be taken,
and retired; nothing could be found but a pig or a cow or
some other animal which had escaped the fire. One place
was their metropolis, and all streamed into this. Round it
was a very deep ravine, and the approaches to the place were
difficult. The light troops went ahead of the heavies half a
mile or more, and crossed the ravine. They saw many sheep
and other animals, and assaulted the stronghold, followed
by large numbers of those who came to forage, spear in
hand, so that those who crossed numbered more than two
thousand men. They could not take the place by assault, for
there was a broad moat round it too, supported by a bank,
with stakes on the banks, and wooden turrets in a row close
together; so they tried to retire, but the enemy fell on them.
To run for it was impossible, for the path down from the
place was only enough for single file. So they sent to Xenophon, who was leading the heavies.

The man came up, and said, "Here's a place full of stuff,
but we can't take it, the place is too strong; and we can't
get away, for they have come out, they are fighting, and
the road down is difficult."

Xenophon on hearing this marched to the ravine, and
ordered the heavy troops to ground arms. He crossed himself with the officers, and considered whether it was better
to bring back those who had crossed, or to bring over the

heavy troops also if he thought the place could be taken. To bring the first men back, he believed, would cost many lives; they all thought the place could be taken, and Xenophon consented to try, trusting the omens: for the seers had declared that there would be a battle, but the issue good in the end.

So he sent the officers to bring the heavy troops over; and moved away the light troops himself, and forbade all long-distance shooting. He told the commanders each to arrange his own companies as he thought they would fight best; for there, side by side, were officers who had been fighting in rivalry for the honours all these long months.

Accordingly they did so; and he ordered the targeteers to carry javelin on strap, and the bowmen to hold arrow on string, ready to let fly at the signal; and the light troops were to fill their pouches with stones. He appointed the proper men to see after all this; and when all was ready, when the lieutenants and petty officers, and the men who thought themselves as good as anyone, had been arranged, they watched each other carefully—for the line was crescent-shaped to fit the place: then they chanted the battle-hymn, and the trumpet sounded, they cheered Eleleu! eleleu! and the heavy troops charged at the double, and missiles flew—spears, arrows, slingstones, showers of stones flung by hand, and some even carried firebrands. The showers and volleys drove the enemy out of their barricades and towers; so Agasias the Stymphalian laid down his arms and climbed up in only his tunic, and one pulled up another, and others climbed, and they took the fortress, as they believed. Then the targeteers and the light troops rushed in, and took what they could.

Xenophon stood by the gate, and kept all the heavy troops outside as far as he could, for other enemies appeared on certain strong high places. Not very long after there was a noise inside, and men came running out with what they had taken, now and then one wounded; there was a great crush at the gate. The fugitives questioned reported that there were heights in the place, and crowds of enemies who sallied out and attacked the men within.

Then he ordered Tolmides the herald to cry, "Anyone who wants spoil, inside!" Numbers went in; they managed to push in, and overpowered the sallying parties and drove the enemy back to their citadel. So outside the citadel all was despoiled; and the heavy-armed men stood easy, some round the breastworks, some by the road leading to the citadel. Xenophon and the captains considered whether it was possible to take the citadel, for that was certain safety, else it seemed very difficult to get away. They examined the place, and thought it impossible to take.

Then they prepared the retreat. Each party demolished the stockade nearest themselves; and they sent away the useless men, and those who had loads of stuff, and most of the heavy troops, and the captains left behind those whom they trusted most.

But when the retreat began, crowds of the enemy sallied out armed with wicker shields, and greaves, and Paphlagonian helmets; parties took possession of the houses on both sides of the way that led to the citadel, so that it was no longer safe even to pursue towards the gate that led to the citadel. For the enemy threw down great baulks of wood, so that it was dangerous both to stay and to go; and the following night was terrible. While they fought thus in great straits, some providence gave them a way of escape; for suddenly a house blazed up on the right, kindled by someone or other; when this collapsed, the men cleared out of the houses on the right. Xenophon heard of this bit of luck, and gave orders to set on fire the left-hand houses too, which were all made of wood; so they were soon burning, and the men ran out of these also. Those at their front were now the only trouble, and these clearly meant to fall on the retreat and the descent.

Then he gave orders to all out of range to collect wood and put it between themselves and the enemy. When there was enough, they set it alight, and they set fire also to the houses along the barricade itself, to give the enemy something to do there. So they escaped with difficulty from the place by making this fire between themselves and the enemy. The whole city was burnt, houses and turrets and barricades and all, everything except the citadel.

Next day the Hellenes retired with their provisions. But they still feared the road down to Trapezûs, which was steep and narrow, so they laid a pretended ambush. A Mysian man (named Mysos himself) took ten Cretans and stayed behind in a bushy place, pretending to wait for the enemy unseen, but their shields were allowed to show again and again, being made of bright metal. The enemy could see this, and feared an ambuscade, and meanwhile the army went down. When they seemed to have gone far enough, a signal was made for Mysos to come back as fast as he could; and the party got up to retreat.

The Cretans thought they would be caught if they ran, so they plunged out of the road into the wood, and rolled down over the rocks and saved themselves; but Mysos ran along the road shouting "Help!" A party went to help him, and found him wounded; then they retreated themselves with the enemy on their heels shooting at them, and some of the Cretans were with them shooting back. So they all returned safe to camp.

III

Cheirisophos did not return, and they could not collect vessels enough, and they could no longer find provisions; so it was decided to go. They put on board the ships those who were sick, those over forty years of age, the boys and women, and all the baggage which was not absolutely necessary for themselves. All these they put in the charge of Philesios and Sophainetos, the oldest of the captains, and the others marched; the roads had been made up. The march brought them on the third day to Cerasûs, a Hellenic city on the seaboard, a colony of Sinope in the Colchian country. There they stayed for ten days; there was a review under arms, and their numbers were counted, and proved to be eight thousand six hundred. These were all who survived; the rest had been lost, in fighting, or in the snow, and a few by disease.

There they divided the money taken from captives. The tithe which they reserved for Apollo and Ephesian Artemis was divided again, and each captain took a share to guard for the gods; Neon of Asine took the share of Cheirisophos.

Xenophon from the share which fell to him afterwards dedicated the offering to Apollo which is in the Athenian Treasury[1] at Delphi, and inscribed on it his own name and the name of Proxenos, who died with Clearchos, for he was his friend. The part which was due to Ephesian Artemis he left behind when he went with Agesilaos out of Asia on the expedition against Bœotia.[2] He put it in charge of Megabyzos the sacristan of Artemis, because he was going where he might risk his life; and he instructed him to return it if he came back alive, but if not, to dedicate some offering which he thought would please the goddess. After his banishment, when he had been settled by the Lacedaimonians at Scillos,[3] Megabyzos visited Olympia to see the Games, and returned him the deposit. Xenophon bought with the money a place for the goddess which the god's oracle indicated. This place, as it happened, had a River Selinûs flowing through it, just as at Ephesus the Selinûs River flows beside the temple of Artemis. There are fishes in both, and mussels; and in the estate at Scillos there is

[1] There were small shrines at Delphi and Olympia, called Treasuries, where various states kept their trappings and some dedications. The Athenian Treasury has been rebuilt and stands now on the spot.

[2] 394 B.C. Agesilaos, King of Sparta, was one of Xenophon's great heroes; he wrote his life, and the story of this expedition in the *Hellenica*.

[3] in Elis, near Olympia

game, all the wild animals that are hunted. He built also an altar and a temple from the sacred money, and ever after he tithed the kindly fruits of the earth and made sacrifice to the goddess, and all citizens and neighbours, men and women, shared in the feast. The goddess provided for this fair wheatmeal, bread, wine, dainties, and a portion of the victims sacrificed from the sacred pasture, and of the game too. For there was hunting for that feast; the sons of Xenophon hunted, and the lads from the place, and anyone else might join in; game was got from the sacred place, and from Mount Pholoë too,[1] pig and gazelle and deer. The district lies on the road from Lacedaimon to Olympia, two or three miles from the temple of Zeus at Olympia. In the sacred estate there is meadowland, and hills covered with wood, suited for breeding pigs and goats and horses, so that even the sumpter animals of those coming to the feast have a feast of their own. Round about the temple a grove of cultivated trees has been planted, all that bear fruit in their season. The temple is made to resemble that in Ephesus, as little to great, and the image made of cypress wood is like the golden one at Ephesus. A pillar stands by the temple with these words engraved:

"THIS PLACE IS SACRED TO ARTEMIS. HE THAT OWNS AND ENJOYS IT SHALL OFFER THE TITHE EACH YEAR: WITH THE RESIDUE HE SHALL KEEP UP THE TEMPLE. WHOSOEVER NEGLECTS THIS, THE GODDESS WILL SEE TO HIM."

IV

From Cerasûs they passed on, those on board ship by sea, the others by land. When they reached the boundaries of the Mossynoicoi, or Wigwam-lodgers, they sent to this tribe Timesitheos the Trapezuntian, who was their public friend or patron at Trapezûs, to ask whether they should pass through the country as enemies or as friends. The answer was, that they should not pass at all; for they relied

---

[1] near the place

on their strongholds. Then Timesitheos told the Hellenes that the tribe on the farther side was an enemy of these, so it was thought well to invite them to an alliance, if they wished. Timesitheos was therefore sent, and brought back their chiefs. The Hellenic captains and the chiefs then met. Xenophon spoke, with Timesitheos as interpreter:

"Gentlemen of the Mossynoicoi, we wish to return safely to Hellas; we must go by land, for we have no ships, and those people are in the way, who we hear are enemies of yours. Then if it is your pleasure, you may have us for allies and punish them for any wrong they have done you, and make them obedient to you for the future. If you let this chance go, consider where you could get such a power to help you again."

The chief of the Mossynoicoi replied that they were in agreement and welcomed the alliance.

"Very well," said Xenophon. "How will you wish to use us if we become allies? And how will you be able to help us on our way home?"

They said, "We are able to invade the country of our enemies and yours on the other side, and to send you vessels here, and men to support you and guide you through the country."

On these terms they exchanged pledges and went. Next day they returned with three hundred dugouts and three men in each; two disembarked and joined the ranks, the third remained, and these paddled off their boats, while the others formed up as I will describe. They stood in rows opposite each other, about a hundred in each; all carried wicker shields faced with hairy white oxhide, shaped like an ivy leaf, and in the right hand a lance of six cubits or so, with a blade in front and a round wooden knob behind. They wore short shirts not quite reaching to the knees, about as thick as sackcloth; and on their heads caps of skin like the Paphlagonians, with a tuft in the middle very much the shape of the tiara. They had also battle-axes of iron. Next, one led and the rest all followed singing in rhythm, and passing through the ranks of the Hellenes and their camp, they set out straight for the enemy to attack a stronghold which they thought most open to attack. This lay in front of the city which they call their metropolis, where is the highest fortress of the Wigwam-lodgers. This was really what the war was about; for whoever held it were considered to be masters of all the Wigwam-lodgers; those who then held it (so people said) had no right to it, as it was common property which they had seized out of greediness.

Some of the Hellenes followed these for plunder, not on duty. As they approached the enemy did nothing at first; but when they were close to the stronghold they rushed out and routed them and killed a number of the natives and a few Hellenes. They pursued until they saw the Hellenes coming up in support; then they retreated, and cutting off the heads of the dead, shook them at the Hellenes and their own enemies, and off they went singing some tune or other.

The Hellenes were very indignant that these men had made the enemy bolder, and that those of themselves who had been with them ran away, although they were a good many: a thing which had never happened before in the whole expedition. Xenophon assembled the Hellenes and said:

"Soldiers, do not be downhearted at what has happened. There is as much good as bad in it, let me tell you. First, you knew that our guides are really enemies to the people who must be our enemies too. Next, you know that those who were careless of discipline and union with us, and thought they could do the same with natives by their side as they can do with us by their side, have been punished for that: in future, then, they will be less likely to be slack in discipline again. Now then, your part is now to prepare yourselves to show the friendly natives that you are better than they are, and to show the enemy that it is not the same thing to fight disciplined men as to fight a disorderly mob."

That day, then, they stayed there. On the next day they sacrificed with good omens; and so after breakfasting, they formed the companies in column and posted the natives on the left in the same order and marched. The bowmen were between the companies, a little behind the head of the heavy-armed men, because some of the enemy's most active troops ran down and pelted them with stones. These were held up by the bowmen and the targeteers, and the others marched along steadily against the stronghold, where on the day before the natives and those with them were routed. There the enemy were drawn up to meet them. The natives stood up to the targeteers and fought them, but when the heavy troops came near they turned; the targeteers chased them right up to the town, and the heavies followed in column. As soon as they were up beside the houses of the metropolis all the enemy massed together and fought, casting their light lances, and holding other spears very heavy and thick, each almost too heavy for a man; and they tried to keep them off with these hand to hand. But the Hellenes did not yield; they went pushing on, and then the natives turned to flight and all left the stronghold. But their king sat still in his mossyn, or wigwam lodge, which was built on the top of the height: there he stays and there they keep him at the public expense. He refused to come out, and so did the one in the stronghold first captured, so they were burnt on the spot with their mossyns.

The Hellenes ransacked the places, and found in the houses stores of loaves in piles, last year's loaves, as the Wigwam-lodgers said, and the fresh corn stored in the straw; most of it was spilt. Besides, slices of dolphin were found in large jars, dried, and dolphin blubber in pottles, which the Wigwam-lodgers used as we use olive oil; plenty of nuts were in the attics, the broad ones with no division.[1] Most of these and most of the corn they boiled and then baked into bread. Wine also was found, which when neat tasted very sharp from its dryness, but with water it was fragrant and pleasant.

Then the Hellenes took breakfast and marched on, leaving the stronghold to the Wigwam-lodgers who had fought with them. They passed many strongholds of those on the enemy side. Those which were easiest of access were either deserted or surrendered without resistance, and these were most of them. The cities were eight or ten miles apart, more or less; when they shouted they could hear each other from city to city, so high were the hills, so deep the valleys. When they were among friends in this march the people held shows for them of rich men's children, fatted children fed on boiled chestnuts, tender and very white, and almost as broad as they were long, with backs and breasts variegated and tattooed all over in flower patterns. They ran after the women in the camp and wanted to lie with them in broad daylight, which was their own custom. All the men and women were fair-skinned. The army said that these were the most savage of all they had seen in their travels, and the farthest away from Hellenic customs. They would do in public what human beings would do in private, and when they were alone they did what people do in company, talk to themselves and laugh at themselves, stop and dance anywhere as if they were showing off.

v

Through this country, hostile and friendly, the Hellenes marched eight stages, and then came to the Chalybes or Ironmen. These are few, and subject to the Wigwam-lodgers, and most of their living comes from working iron.

[1] chestnuts, not walnuts

Then they reached the Tibarenians. Their country was more level, and they had forts near the sea, not so strong. The captains wished to attack these places and get a bit in pocket, so they refused the gifts which were offered and told them to wait until they had deliberated. They sacrificed, and the seers after many sacrifices declared one and all that the gods did not at all approve of war. Then they accepted the gifts of friendship, and marching as through friendly country for two days reached Cotyora, a Hellenic city, a colony of Sinope, which is in the Tibyrenian country.[1]

They stayed forty-five days. In this time they offered sacrifices to the gods, and made procession, each nation of the Hellenic race by itself, and held games and sports. They got their provisions partly from Paphlagonia, partly from the villages of the district, for they would neither give them a market nor allow the sick to be brought within their walls.

After a while an embassy came from Sinope; Cotyora was their city and paid them tribute, so they were anxious about the city, and the country also, which they heard was being raided. They came to the camp for a parley; their spokesman was Hecatonymos, reputed to be an accomplished orator, and he said:

"We are sent to you, soldiers and gentlemen, by the city of Sinope, to congratulate you Hellenes as victors over barbarians; and to say we rejoice with you that, after so many great dangers, as we have heard, you are with us safe and sound. We are Hellenes, and you are Hellenes, and we expect from you no unkindness but some kindness. These men of Cotyora are colonists of ours; this country we have taken from barbarians and given to them, and they in return pay us tribute like Cerasûs and Trapezûs, so that if you do any harm to them the city of Sinope considers this as done to herself. Now we hear that some of you have violently entered the city and there made yourselves at home

---

[1] A footnote has been added in the text calculating the distance traversed at 620 leagues. Time taken, eight months.

in the houses, and that you take what you want from the farms by force, not by consent. We do not think that right. If you will do that, we must needs make friends with Corylas and the Paphlagonians and anyone else we can find."

In answer to this, Xenophon rose and spoke for the army: "We also, gentlemen of Sinope, are well content that we have come through with our lives and our arms all safe; for it is impossible at one time both to fight our enemies and to plunder their goods and chattels. And now we have reached the cities of our own race. Well, at Trapezûs a market was given us, and we paid for our provisions, and for their good respect and the hospitable gifts they gave to the army we respected them in return, and kept our hands off all friends they had among the natives; as for their enemies, they led us themselves against them, and we did them whatever damage we could. Ask them what manner of men they found us; for some of them are here, whom that city sent with us in friendship as guides.

"Wherever we come and get no market, whether barbarian country or Hellenic, we take our provisions, not from brutality but from necessity. Kurds and Taochians and Chaldeans, although they are not subjects of the king, and although they are formidable, we treated as enemies because of the necessity of getting provisions, since they would give no market. The Macronians were not able to provide a market, but although they are barbarians we considered them to be friends, and took from them nothing by force. But these men of Cotyora, who you say are yours—if we have taken anything from them, they are responsible themselves; for they did not behave as friends to us, but they closed their gates. They refused to let us in, and sent no market out. They professed that the governor appointed by you was responsible. You say we went in by force and made ourselves at home there; but we asked them to receive our sick and wounded under shelter, and when they would not open their gates, we walked in where the place itself gave us leave. We did nothing else by force, but our sick are quartered in houses under shelter, and paying their own expenses, in order that our sick may not be at your governor's mercy but we may fetch them out when we wish. The rest of us, as you see, are encamped under the sky, and in military order, prepared to defend themselves if attacked, and to treat as friends those who treat us as friends.

"You have threatened to make Corylas and the Paphlagonians allies against us if it is your pleasure; well, we will fight you both, if there is any necessity. We have already fought others many times more numerous than you; and if it is our pleasure to make the Paphlagonian himself our ally (we hear that he covets both your city and the places on the coast), we will try to be friends to him in helping him to what he covets."

It was clear after this that the other ambassadors were very angry with Hecatonymos for what he said; and one of them rose and said:

"We have come, not to declare war, but to prove we are friends. If you will come to Sinope, we will receive you there with hospitable gifts; and now we will ask the inhabitants to give what they can, for we see that all you have said is true."

Then the people of Cotyora sent gifts of hospitality, and the captains entertained the ambassadors of Sinope; all talked together in the most friendly way, and particularly each inquired what the others wanted about the rest of their march.

VI

On this day the matter ended so; and on the next the captains called a meeting of the soldiers. They decided to call in the ambassadors and consult about their march onwards. If they must go by land, they thought friends at

Sinope might be useful, since they knew all about Paphlagonia; they would need them all the more if they went by
sea, for only they seemed able to provide vessels enough for
the army. Accordingly they invited the ambassadors to give
their counsel, and they called on them, as fellow-countrymen, to begin their good entertainment by showing goodwill and giving good advice.

Hecatonymos rose first, and gave an apology for what he
had said about making friends with the Paphlagonian; he
did not mean they were going to make war upon the Hellenes, but only that it was in their power to make friends
with the barbarians, and they chose the Hellenes. Since they
asked his advice, he called thus upon Heaven: "If I advise
what I believe to be best, may all good befall me: if not, I
pray the opposite. This seems to be a case of what they call
'sacred counsel' [1]: for now assuredly if I prove to have given
good advice, many will commend me; if bad advice, many
will curse me. I know that there will be much more trouble
for us if you go by sea, for we shall have to provide the vessels; but if you journey by land, you will have to be the fight-
ers. Nevertheless, I must say what my judgment is, for I
know the Paphlagonian country and its power. It contains
both splendid plains and most lofty mountains.

"And in the first place I know exactly where it is necessary
to make entry. No other entry is possible, except one where
the horns of the mountains are high above each side of the
road; get hold of these, and a few men could keep the pass,
but if these are held, all the men in the world would be
unable to pass. I could show you the place, if you would
send someone with me. Secondly, I know that there are
plains, and cavalry which the barbarians themselves believe
to be stronger than all the king's cavalry. Just lately the king
summoned them and they would not go; their governor
is too proud. And even if you can steal your way through,
or seize the heights first, and on the plain if you conquer

[1] which must be true: a proverb

their horse, and their foot more than a hundred and twenty thousand, you will come to the rivers.

"First, the Thermodon,[1] 300 feet wide, which I believe to be difficult to cross, especially in the face of so many enemies; second, the Iris,[2] also 300 feet; third, the Halys,[3] not less than a quarter of a mile, which I think you could not cross without boats—and who will give you boats? So also the Parthenis[4] is impassable, and you will come to that if you cross the Halys. Therefore I think the land way is not only difficult for you but wholly impossible. But if you go by water you can coast along to Sinope, and from Sinope to Heracleia; from Heracleia neither land nor water is impracticable, for there is plenty of shipping at Heracleia."

When he had finished, some suspected he spoke in friendship for Corylas, for he was his national friend at Sinope. Some, that he expected a handsome reward for this advice. Some suspected that he feared they might damage the Sinopean country if they went by land. But in any case the public vote was in favour of going by sea.

After this Xenophon said, "Gentlemen of Sinope, the men have chosen the journey by sea which you advise. Then the matter stands thus: if there shall be shipping enough, so that not one shall be left here, we will go by water; but if some of us are to be left and some sail, we will not go on board. For we understand that where we are masters, there we can get provisions and save our lives too; but if we shall be caught anywhere weaker than our enemies, it is plain as daylight that we shall be so many slaves."

On hearing this, the ambassadors asked them to send men to deal with the question. They chose Callimachos the Arcadian, and Ariston the Athenian, and Samolas the Achaian; and they departed.

Meanwhile Xenophon looked upon all these men-at-arms, and all those targeteers, and the bowmen and slingers

[1] Thermeh
[3] Kizil-Irmak
[2] Yeshil-Irmak
[4] Chati-Su

and horsemen, too, and all fit from long practice—he saw all these on the Euxine, where so great a force could never have been collected without vast expense, and he thought it would be fine to found a city there, and to add territory and power to Hellas. It would be a grand place, he thought, when he calculated their numbers and all the people living about that sea. But before he told anyone, he called up Silanos the Ambraciot, who had been seer to Cyros, and made sacrifice in consideration of this design. But Silanos was afraid this might be done, and the army might remain somewhere; so he spread the tale through the army that Xenophon wished the army to remain and to found a city, and get a great name and power for himself. Silanos wanted to get back to Hellas as soon as possible; for he had kept safe the 3,000 darics which Cyros gave him, when he was right about the ten days at that sacrifice.[1]

Some of the soldiers were willing to obey when they heard the tale, but most were not. Timasion the Dardanian and Thorax the Bœotian told some merchants from Sinope and Heracleia who were present that if they would not find pay for the men, so that they could get food on board ship, there was a risk that all this great force might remain on the Euxine. "Xenophon wants it," they said, "and he begs us to say suddenly to the men when the vessels are here, 'Look here, men, you see we are in a fix now to get provisions for the voyage home, and a few little presents for our people when we get home. If you like, just choose any place you fancy in the inhabited country round the sea here, where you would like to settle. Then go home if you like, stay if you like: there are your ships, choose wherever you like and just pounce on the place.' "

The merchants reported this rumour in their cities; Timasion the Dardanian sent two men, Eurymachos the Dardanian and Thorax the Bœotian, to say the same. Then the people of those two cities sent someone with a present

[1] see p. 23

for Timasion, if he would arrange that the army should sail. Timasion was pleased to hear this, and when the soldiers were in assembly he spoke to them: "Don't set your hearts on staying here, men: Hellas and home! There's nothing better than that. But I hear some people are looking for lucky omens to stay here, without one word to you. I promise you as soon as you are on board—pay, from the first of the month, a cyzicene [1] per man per month! and I will bring you to the Troad, my own country, although I'm an exile, but they will be glad to see me and they will back you up. I will be your guide, I will take you where you will find plenty of money. I know all about the Aeolid, and Phrygia, and the Troad, and all the empire of Pharnabazos; my home is in those parts, and I served there with Clearchos and Dercylidas."

Then Thorax the Bœotian got up next, who had a quarrel with Xenophon for the chief command; he said that once out of the Euxine there was the Chersonese [2] ready for them, a fine prosperous country if anyone wanted to settle there, or he might go home if he liked. When there was country plenty and to spare in Hellas, it was ridiculous to go poking about among the barbarians. "Until you get there," says he, "I promise you the same pay as Timasion." This he said because he knew what the merchants had promised to Timasion if he cleared them out.

Meanwhile Xenophon said nothing; but two Achaians, Philesios and Lycon, said it was a shame that Xenophon privately advised people to stay, and looked for omens to persuade them to stay, and in public he would say nothing. Thus Xenophon was obliged to get up and speak. He said:

"Gentlemen, I make sacrifice, it is true, and seek omens as you see, to my best ability, for your sakes and for mine, to procure this: I speak and think and do what shall be best for yourselves, and best for me too. And now I have been inquiring on this very point, whether it is better that

[1] a golden coin rather larger than the daric
[2] Gallipoli

I should propose it and try to bring it off, or whether I should not touch the matter at all. Silanos the seer declared that the omens were good, and that's the chief thing. He knew I could tell myself, since I have been present at many a sacrifice. But he reported that the victim showed some plot and intrigue against me. He discovered this really because he was plotting himself to spread slanders against me; for he sent word round that I meant to do this at once without your consent.

"But the truth is, if I saw you in difficulties, I should have inquired how it could be managed that you should take a city; when those who wished might sail at once, and the others might wait until they could get enough to put something in their friends' pockets at home. But now that I see the merchants from Heracleia and Sinope are sending ships to carry you, and people are promising pay from the first of the month, it seems a good chance to come safe where we wish, and be paid for it at the same time. Therefore I give up that plan, and I ask any who have agreed with me to give it up too.

"This is my opinion: While you are here, so many together, I think you will be respected and have your provisions; for power gives plunder of those that are under! But if you are scattered, and your strength is broken into little bits, you could not take and you could not come off scot-free. I agree, then, with you that you should sail for Hellas, but if anyone be found deserting before the whole army is safe, he shall be judged as a criminal. Those who approve hold up your hands." All held up their hands.

But Silanos rose, and tried to say it was fair that anyone should go if he liked. But the men would not let him; they threatened that if they caught him showing his heels he should be punished.

The ships were sent at once from Heracleia as soon as

they knew that the army had voted to go, and that Xenophon himself put it to the vote; but they broke their promise
to Timasion and Thorax that they would find the money.
These men were confounded; they had promised the pay
to the soldiers, and they feared the army. Accordingly they
gathered the other captains who had been in the secret—
these were all except Neon, who was second-in-command
to Cheirisophos, and Cheirisophos was absent still—and
waited on Xenophon. They told him they were sorry, and
they thought it best to sail to Phasis, as they had the ships,
and take the Phasian country; the king there was descended
from Aietes, as it happened. Xenophon replied that he
would not say one word to the army on this matter. "Assemble them yourselves, if you like," says he, "and tell
them." Then Timasion suggested that they should not call
a meeting but each try to persuade his own men. So they
departed and did this.

VII

Soon the soldiers heard of all this confusion. Neon declared that Xenophon had talked over the other captains,
and intended to take the men deceitfully back to Phasis.
The soldiers were indignant; they gathered in clumps and
circles, and there was danger that they might do as they
did to the Colchian heralds and masters of the market—
stoned them all except those who jumped into the sea. But
when Xenophon found out this he decided to summon a
general assembly at once, and not to let them gather in
groups by themselves. So he told the herald to cry meeting;
and the men all assembled readily enough. Then Xenophon did not denounce the captains for applying to him,
but spoke as follows:

"Men, I hear that someone is calumniating me, and saying
that I mean to deceive you, and to sail for Phasis. Hear me,

then, in God's name. If I am proved guilty, I must not leave this place until I am punished; but if these are proved guilty who slander me, treat them as they deserve.

"You know, I suppose, where the sun rises and where he sets. You know that if one is going to sail for Hellas he must steer westwards; if one wishes to sail for barbarian lands he must go back to the east. Then who could deceive you in that? Who could persuade you that the sun sets where he rises, and rises where he sets? And further, you know that the north wind takes you out of the Euxine to Hellas, and the south wind takes you in to Phasis. When the north wind blows, don't they say, Good voyage for Hellas now! Can anyone deceive you in this, then, and make you embark when the south wind blows? Perhaps you think I will put you on board when it is calm. Well, I shall be in one ship, and you in a hundred at least; then how can I compel you to sail with me if you don't want to do it? How could I deceive you and take you off? But I will put it that you *are* deceived and bewitched by me, and you *do* come to Phasis; suppose we do disembark in the country—you will know that this is not Hellas, I suppose? And I the deceiver shall be one: you the deceived nearly ten thousand armed men. Could a man better make sure of his own punishment than by such a plan for himself and for you?

"No, these are the words of men, who are both fools and jealous of me because you respect me. However, they could not fairly find anything in me to make them jealous. When do I hinder any of you from speaking, if you have anything good to say? From fighting if he will for you and himself? From watching and caring for your safety? Come now, when you elect commanders, do I stand in the way of anyone? Let him be commander, I give way: only let him prove he is doing you good.

"Well, that is enough about me: but you—if anyone

believes that he could have been deceived in these things, or that he could deceive another, let him speak, and say how. But when you have had enough of this, do not disperse until you hear what a business I see beginning in this army. If it shall come upon us, and if it shall be what it gives signs of being, it is high time to be careful for ourselves, or we may prove to be the basest and worst of men in the sight of heaven and earth, in the sight of friends and enemies."

When the soldiers heard this they wondered what it could be, and told him to speak. So he began again:

"You remember at Cerasûs there were some native strongholds in the mountains, friendly to Cerasûs, out of which people used to come and sell animals and other things they had; and I think some of you went to the nearest one, and bought things and came back. Captain Clearetos learnt this, and heard it was a small place, and unguarded because they thought themselves friends. So he marched up there at night, to sack the place, without saying a word to any of us. His plan was, if he took the place, not to return to camp, but to embark on a ship, which happened to be offshore with his messmates on board; he was going to put on board what he got, and sail clean away out of the Euxine. His messmates on board had arranged this with him, as I now learn. So he collected those whom he had persuaded to join him, and set out for the place. But day broke before he reached it, the people collected and cast down rocks from strong positions, and killed Clearetos and many more, but some of them escaped to Cerasûs. This happened on the very day when we set out to march here; but some of those who travelled by sea are still at Cerasûs, not yet having set sail.

"After this, as the Cerasuntines say, three of the elders of that little fort came and asked the way to our public assembly. As they could not find us, they complained to the Cerasuntines and asked why we had attacked them. They replied, as they said, that it was no public business; and the men were glad and intended to sail here, in order to record the event and to offer the dead for burial. But some of those who had escaped happened to be still in Cerasûs; when these men discerned where they were going, they had the impudence to pelt them with stones and called others to help. The men were killed, all three, ambassadors, stoned to death. Upon this the Cerasuntines came and told us all about it; and we captains were indignant, and arranged with the Cerasuntines to bury our dead. While we were in session outside the camp we suddenly heard an uproar, and shouts, 'Hit 'em! hit 'em! Shoot 'em! shoot 'em!' and soon we saw a crowd of men running with stones, and others picking up stones. The Cerasuntines retreated to their ships in dismay, as you might expect after what they had seen at home; and some of us were afraid, I can tell you. However, I went and asked what the matter was. Many of them didn't know, but still they had stones in their hands. When I found someone who did, he told me that the market masters were treating the army shamefully. Meanwhile somebody sees Zelarchos, a market master, walking towards the sea, and gives a shout; when the people heard they rushed at him, as if a wild boar or a stag had appeared before them. When the Cerasuntines saw them rushing in their direction they felt sure it was meant for them, and ran away and threw themselves into the sea. Some of our own men jumped in too, and anyone who could not swim was drowned. Now what do you think about these? They had done no harm, they were only afraid that we had gone mad like mad dogs.

"Well, if things like that are to happen, consider what the state of this army will be. You as a whole will not have it in your power either to undertake war or to cease it at your own pleasure, but any single person will lead the army wherever he likes. And if any ambassadors wait on you, asking for peace or anything else, those who wish will kill them, and keep you from hearing those who come to speak to you. Next, those whom you as a whole elect for commanders will be simply nowhere; but whatever single person elects himself commander and chooses to say, 'Shoot 'em, shoot 'em,' he will be able to kill the commander, and any private person among you, if he likes, untried, if he finds followers, as did happen just now.

"Just consider what these self-elected captains have done for you. If Zelarchos the market master has done wrong, he has gone off unpunished; if he has not done wrong, he has run from the army for fear he might be killed unjustly, untried. Those who stoned the ambassadors have arranged matters, so that of all the Hellenes alive, you only cannot enter Cerasûs with safety unless you have a force with you; and those dead whom the very men who killed them offered for burial—for those dead they have arranged matters so, that even a man with a herald's badge will not find it safe to remove them. Who will dare to go as herald after murdering heralds? We had to beg the Cerasuntines to bury them for us.

"Very well, if you are satisfied with this, pass a vote to say so; and then we shall know where we are, and each one will keep his own guard, and be careful to occupy the heights commanding his own tent. However, if any of you think that these are the doings of wild beasts, not of human beings, see how you can stop them. Or else, good God, how shall we make solemn sacrifice when we gladly do impious deeds? How shall we fight our enemies if we kill each other off? What city will receive us in friendship when it sees lawlessness like this among us? Who will provide a market in confidence if we are seen to commit great offences like these? And that universal fame which we expect—who would say even a word of praise for such men? No, I am sure they would say that those who do such things are a bad lot."

Then they all rose like one man, and said that those who had begun this business must be punished, and for the future no lawlessness was to be allowed: anyone who began it should be tried for his life; the captains were to bring all to trial, and the court should hear all complaints from the death of Cyros onwards, and the captains were to be a board of judges. Xenophon pleaded, and the seers advised, that the army should be purified, and there was a purification.

VIII

It was decided that the captains also be brought under scrutiny for the time past. Philesios was condemned, and Xanthicles, for the custody of the cargoes from the barges, to pay the deficit, twenty minae; Sophainetos, a fine of ten minae because, being elected to some office, he neglected his duty. Xenophon was accused by some men, who said he had struck them, and made a charge of assault and battery.

Xenophon asked the first who spoke to say where he had been assaulted. He answered, "Where we were freezing to death and there was all that snow." Xenophon said, "Oh dear, oh dear! In all that storm, no food to eat, not even a smell of wine, fainting for hardship, enemy following—if at a time like that I committed assault and battery, then I was a lewd fellow of the baser sort, and lewder than a jackass, who never gets tired of it, as they say. However, go on, tell us how you came to be beaten. Did I ask you for something, and you said No, and I beat you? Or ask you to pay up a debt? Did I make love to you? Was I drunk and worked it off on you?" He said No to all these; and Xenophon asked if he was man-at-arms? No, said he. Targeteer? No, he said again, not that, but his messmates fixed

on him to drive a mule, though he was not a slave. Then
Xenophon remembered the man, and asked, "Are you the
one who carried the sick man?" "Yes, by God," he said,
"for you made me, and you scattered my mates' goods all
over the place." "Oh well," said Xenophon, "this was the
scattering. I gave the things round to others and told them
to return it all to me, received it, and gave you the whole
safe, when you had reported to me with the man. Now
listen, all, and hear what happened; it's worth while. A
man was being left behind because he could not walk. I
made this man carry him that he might not perish, for the
enemy were close upon us, I think." The fellow agreed.
"Then," said Xenophon, "when I had sent you on, I came
and found you again with the rearguard, digging a hole
to bury the man, as it seemed, and I stood there and praised
you. While we stood there, the man crooked his leg, and
they shouted out, 'The man's alive!' and you said, 'Alive
as much as he likes, anyhow I won't carry him.' Then I
struck you, that's quite true, for I thought you knew well
enough he was alive." "What then?" says he, "was he any
the less dead after I reported to you and showed him?"
"Oh yes," Xenophon said, "we shall all die, but is that any
reason why we should be buried alive?" Then there was
a shout, "A pity he did not give him a few more!"

After that Xenophon asked the others to say in what
place each had been beaten. No-one stood up, and Xenophon went on, "I admit, gentlemen, that I have really beaten
certain persons for bad discipline, men who were content
to let you save their lives when you kept your places and
fought where it was your duty, and then they left their
places and ran on to plunder and to cheat you. If we had
all done that, we should all have perished. Yes, and I have
beaten a man before now for playing the softie, when he
would not get up, and just threw himself away to the enemy,
and I have forced him to march. In that awful weather I

once sat myself for a long time, while I waited for some men who were packing up, and I found out how hard it was to get up again and stretch my legs. So I learnt from my own experience, and whenever I saw someone sitting idle I drove him on; for to move and be a man gave some warmth and suppleness, but to sit still, I saw, only helped to freeze the blood and rot off the toes, which you know yourselves happened to many. Another, perhaps, who lingered only to rest somewhere, and hindered both you in front and us behind from marching, I have struck with a fist, that an enemy might not strike him with a spear. Well, now their lives have been saved they can have justice done on me, if I have done them anything contrary to justice. If they had come into the enemy's hands, what wrong would they have suffered so great that they could expect now to have justice?

"My defence is simple," said he. "If I have chastised anyone for his own good, I claim to defend myself as a father to a son, or a schoolmaster to a boy. Indeed, doctors even burn and cut for one's good. If you think a love of violence made me do it, consider that now, thank God, I am more confident than then, I am bolder now than then, I drink more wine now, yet I strike no-one: for I see you all in fine weather. But when a storm comes, and a great sea threatens, don't you notice that only a shake of the head makes the prowsman angry with those in the prow, and the helmsman angry with those at the stern? Yes, for in such a crisis the smallest errors may ruin all.

"But you have already decided that I did right in striking those men. There you stood, holding swords, not voting-tables, and you could have protected them if you wished; but you did not protect them, nor indeed, I confess, did you join me in striking them. So far you did give liberty to the cowardly men among them by leaving them alone. For I believe, if you care to inquire, that the greatest cowards then are the most violent now. At least, Boïscos the Thessalian boxer, how hard he fought then not to carry that shield! Said he was tired! But now, as I hear, he has stript many men of Cotyora to the skin! Then if you are prudent, you will treat him the opposite way to a dog. Dangerous dogs are chained up in the day and let loose at night; you will let this man loose in the day, and, if you are prudent, chain him up at night.

"But really," said he, "I am surprised that you remember every time that I made myself disagreeable to one of you. No silence there, no; but if I sheltered anyone from cold, or saved anyone from an enemy, or found something for a sick man, or someone in a fix, nobody remembers that; and you do not remember if I praised anyone for doing a job well, or honoured a brave man where I could. Yet it is just and holy and pleasant to remember good things rather than bad."

When he finished, they began to call up their memories, and all ended well.

BOOK SIX

After this, while the delay lasted, they lived partly from the market and partly by making raids on Paphlagonia. The Paphlagonians, too, were quite clever at kidnapping stragglers, and they tried to damage those who were camped far out; in consequence, both sides were bitterly hostile. At last Corylas, who then was the ruler of Paphlagonia, sent ambassadors to the Hellenes, bringing horses and fine apparel, and offered to make an agreement between them, to live and let live. The captains answered that they must deliberate with the army, but they offered hospitality, and invited those of their own friends who seemed to have the best right. They killed some of the captured cattle and other victims, and made a sacrifice and a sufficient banquet. They dined reclining on their low beds, and drinking from the horn cups which they found in the country.

When libation had been made, and they had chanted the hymn, first Thracians got up and danced to the pipes fully armed, leaping high and lightly and using their swords; at last one struck another, and all thought he really wounded him, but the man only fell in a clever way on purpose; and the Paphlagonians shrieked aloud. The other stript off his arms, and went out singing the Sitalcas[1]; others of the Thracians carried him out like a corpse, but he had no harm.

After this the Ainianians and Magnesians rose, and danced in full armour what they call the Harvest Song. The method of dancing is, that one lays down his arms, and sows, and drives the plow, turning again and again as in fear. A raider approaches; the other looks out, and picks up his arms, and goes to meet him, and fights in front of the yoke. These also did their play in time with the pipes. At last the raider ties up his man and drives the oxen away; or sometimes the plowman ties up the raider, and then fastens him beside the oxen, and drives him with hands fastened behind his back.

After this a Mysian came in with a light shield in each hand. Sometimes he danced in mimicry of two men fighting; sometimes he used the shields as if against one, and then he twirled about and threw somersaults out of the door holding the shields, and a rare good show it was. At last he danced the Persian, clashing the shields together, crouching and jumping up; and all this he did in time with the pipes.

Next Mantineans and other Arcadians rose, arrayed in their finest accoutrements, and, keeping time with the pipes, did the march-at-arms, and chanted their hymn, and danced as they do in processionals before the gods.

When the Paphlagonians saw these, they said how strange it was that all the dances were done under arms. The Mysian saw their astonishment, and persuaded an Arcadian, who owned a dancing-girl, to dress her in her finery, and let him bring her in with a light shield in her hand. She danced the Pyrrhic daintily. Then there was loud applause, and the Paphlagonians asked if these women fought by their

---

[1] the national hymn, named after the national hero

side. They said yes, it was the women who drove the Great King out of camp. This was the end of that night.

Next day the captains introduced them to the army. The soldiers voted for peace between them. Live and let live. After this the Paphlagonians went away, and the Hellenes, as there seemed to be shipping enough ready, embarked, and sailed a day and a night before a good wind, keeping Paphlagonia on the left. The day after, they reached Sinope, and anchored in Harmene, a port of Sinope. The city lies in Paphlagonia, but they are a colony from Miletos.

They sent out gifts of welcome, barley-meal three thousand measures,[1] wine fifteen hundred jars. Cheirisophos was there too, with a ship of war. The soldiers expected him to have something for them, but he had nothing; he said only that Admiral Anaxibios and the others sent their congratulations, and Anaxibios promised that if they came out of the Euxine there should be pay for them.

In this port of Harmene they stayed five days. Being now so near to Hellas, they felt more than ever anxious to come home with something in their pockets. They thought that the best thing would be to choose one commander; for one man could manage the army better than many, and use it by night or day; if they had to be secret, things would be hidden better; and if they must be first, one is less likely to be too late, for there would be no need of discussion, but the opinion of the one would be carried out. Hitherto the captains had decided everything by a majority.

With this notion they turned to Xenophon. The captains approached him, and said that was the judgment of the army; and each of them with the greatest goodwill pressed him to undertake the command.

Xenophon was inclined for many reasons to accept. He thought that his honour would be greater among his friends, and his reputation would be greater in his native city, and

[1] each about 1½ bushels

perhaps it might benefit the army. These thoughts made him wish to be sole plenipotentiary commander. But when he remembered that no man can forsee how the future will turn out, and thus there was danger that he might lose even the reputation he had, he was in doubt. In his perplexity he thought it best to lay the matter before the gods above and let them decide.

He provided two victims, and made sacrifice to Zeus the King, the god to whom the oracle at Delphi had bidden him sacrifice [1]; and he it was had sent the dream, so he believed, which he saw when he began to take part in the business of the army. And at the time when he set out from Ephesus to be introduced to Cyros, he remembered an eagle which had screamed on the right, yet still sitting; and the seer who was escorting him said that this was a great omen, and proper for a great man, full of glory and yet full of hardship, for the other birds are most ready to attack the eagle when sitting; however, not an omen of profit, for the eagle takes his provender on the wing rather than sitting. When he made this sacrifice, the god signified quite clearly that he was neither to ask for further command nor accept it if they should elect him.

So things were when the army assembled, and all voted to elect one; when this was decided, they proposed Xenophon. Since it was clear that they meant to elect him, if it were put to the vote, he rose and spoke as follows:

"Gentlemen, I am but human, and I cannot help being pleased to be honoured by you. I thank you, and I pray the gods to grant that I may be the cause of some good for you. But to prefer me as your commander when a man of Lacedaimon is present seems to be neither profitable to you nor to me: you would be less likely to win anything from them if you have need; and for me I think such a thing is not very safe. For I see that they never ceased fighting against my own native city, until the whole city was compelled to

[1] see p. 59

admit that Lacedaimon was the leader: but as soon as they did admit that, they ceased fighting at once and besieged the city no longer. Then, if seeing this I should annul this high claim of theirs, as far as in me lies, I have a notion I might be taught a lesson too quickly. As to your own notion, that there would be less faction with me commander than with many, be sure that if you elect another you will not find me leading a faction; for I think that he who leads faction against his commander in war leads faction against his own life. But if you elect me, I should not be surprised if you should find someone angry both with you and with me."

When he finished many more got up and said that he ought to be commander; and Agasias the Stymphalian said it would be ridiculous if things really were as he described. "Will Lacedaimon fly into a rage if a dinner party does not put a Lacedaimonian in the chair? If things really are so," says he, "we can't be officers, because we are Arcadians!" Loud applause followed; they thought that good. Xenophon saw that something more was necessary, and he rose and said, "Well, gentlemen, I must tell you the whole truth, on my oath by all the gods and goddesses in heaven. I made sacrifice to inquire whether it was better for you to entrust this command to me, and for me to accept; and the gods gave such manifest signs in the victims, that even an ignoramus could see I must hold aloof from sole command!"

After this they elected Cheirisophos; and Cheirisophos, elected, rose up and said, "At least I will assure you, gentlemen, that I would have made no faction myself if you had elected another; however, as regards Xenophon, you were kind to him not to elect him, for as it is, Dexippos [1] has been running him down to Anaxibios, although I told him to shut up. He said Xenophon would rather share command of Clearchos's force with a Dardanian, Timasion, than

[1] see p. 162

with himself, a Laconian. However, since you have chosen me," says he, "I also will try my best to do you some good. Then you must all make ready to set sail to-morrow, if there is good weather. We shall sail to Heracleia, so you must do your best to make anchorage there. What next, we will consider when we get there."

II

From that place next day they set sail before a good wind, and for two days they coasted. As they sailed along the coast they had seen Jason's Beach,[1] where the Argo is said to have moored; and the mouths of the rivers, first Thermodon, then Iris, then Halys, then Parthenios, and lastly they reached Heracleia, a Hellenic city and a colony of Megara, lying in the country of the Mariandynians. So they anchored by the Acherusian Chersonese, where Heracles is said to have gone down for the Dog Cerberos; and there they still show the marks of his descent, a cleft more than four hundreds yards deep. There the people sent gifts of hospitality from Heracleia, barley meal three thousand measures, and wine two thousand jars, twenty oxen, and a hundred sheep. There is a river running across the plain, named Lycos, width about two hundred feet.

The soldiers met and debated whether to go on by land or sea out of the Euxine. Lycon the Achaian rose and said:

"I am surprised, gentlemen, at our commanders; they do not try to get provisions for us, for these gifts are not three days' food for the army. Where to get food for our journey I don't know," says he. "I propose, then, that we demand from Heracleia not less than three thousand cyzicenes." Another proposed not less than ten thousand; that ambassadors should be chosen on the spot, and that the army should stay while the ambassadors went to the city to see what offers were made, and decide accordingly.

Then they put forward as ambassadors, first Cheirisophos,

[1] Yasoun Bouroun

because he was commander, and some added Xenophon. They opposed strongly; both agreed that they ought not to force from a Hellenic city, and a friend, what they did not offer willingly. Since these two were not so minded they sent Lycon the Achaian and a Parrhasian Callimachos and Agasias the Stymphalian. Those went and told the resolutions, and Lycon added threats, as was said, if they should refuse. The Heracleots replied that they would deliberate; and at once they brought in everything from the farms, and made their market inside, and shut the gates, and arms could be seen on the walls.

Then those who had made this mess laid the blame on their captains, who had spoilt the business, as they said. The Arcadians and the Achaians joined forces, under the ringleaders Callimachos and Lycon. They said it was a shame that Peloponnesians should be commanded by an Athenian and a Lacedaimonian who had brought no force to the army; they had the work themselves, and others had the profits, and that, too, although they had saved the army themselves; Arcadians and Achaians had done it, the rest of the army was nothing (and in truth Arcadians and Achaians were more than half the army): then if they had common sense, they would join and elect their own captains for themselves, and go on by themselves, and try to make a good job of it. This was decided. Any Arcadians or Achaians that were under Cheirisophos and Xenophon left them; they joined together, and elected captains from themselves, ten in number, and voted that each was to do what should be decided by a majority. Thus the sole command of Cheirisophos was ended then and there, a week after he was elected.

However, Xenophon wished to proceed in company with them, which he thought safer than that everyone should go by himself. But Neon persuaded him to go separately; for Cheirisophos had told him that Cleandros, the governor at Byzantium, said he was coming with ships-of-war to Calpe's Haven; he wanted no-one else to share, only they and their own men would have a passage home in these ships, and that was why he gave such advice. Cheirisophos just let him do what he liked; he was in despair at the whole business, and hated the army. Xenophon still wanted to be quit of the army and sail away; but he sacrificed to Leader Heracles and asked his question, whether it were right and good to quit the army with those that remained of his men, or to go on with the army; and the god signified by the omens that he should go with the army. Thus the army was divided into three: Arcadians and Achaians, more than four thousand, all men-at-arms; Cheirisophos with fourteen hundred men-at-arms and seven hundred targeteers, Clearchos's Thracians; and Xenophon with seventeen hundred men-at-arms, and three hundred targeteers—he alone had cavalry, about forty horsemen.

The Arcadians managed to get ships from Heracleia, and sailed away first. They wished to make a sudden descent on Bithynia, and get as much as possible, and they landed at Calpe's Haven [1] somewhere in the middle of the Thracian coast. Cheirisophos marched by land from Heracleia, at first through the country, but when he came to Thrace he kept along the seashore, for he was ill. Xenophon took ship to the boundaries of Thrace and the Heracleiotid, and went on across country.

III

We will follow each party. The Arcadians landed by night in Calpe's Haven, and marched to the first villages, about eight miles from the sea. At dawn each captain led his own company to a village; two went together if the village appeared to be large. They arranged a rendezvous on a hill; and by their sudden assault they took many captives and surrounded large quantities of sheep. But the

[1] Karpe Liman

Thracians who escaped gathered together; and very many did escape with their light shields clean out of the hands of the heavy troops. When these had assembled, first they attacked the company of Smicres, one of the captains, as it was retiring to the rendezvous laden with booty. The Hellenes for a time fought marching, but in crossing a ravine the natives routed them and killed them all with Smicres himself. From the company of Hegesandros, another of the ten captains, they left only eight men, and the captain himself was saved alive. The other companies rendezvoused, some with difficulty and some without; but the Thracians after this great success went round shouting for help and collected in force during the night. At daybreak they mustered round the hill where the Hellenes were encamped, horsemen and targeteers in large numbers, and more were always rolling in. They attacked the heavy troops with complete safety, for the Hellenes had not a bowman, not a javelineer, not a horseman: the natives ran in and rode in and cast their javelins, and when the others attacked they easily escaped, and set on them from all sides. Most of them were wounded, but none of the natives; so they could not stir out of the place, and at last the Thracians cut them off from their water too. In this despair they parleyed for a truce, and they came to some agreement, but the Thracians would not give hostages when the demand was made, and there was the rub. So much for the Arcadians.

Cheirisophos marched safely as far as Calpe's Haven. Xenophon went on his march across country; and on the way his horsemen met some old men going somewhere. These were brought to Xenophon, and he asked if they had noticed another Hellenic force anywhere about. They told him all that had happened, and that they were now encamped on a hill with all the Thracians round them in a ring. Then he put the old men under strict guard, to show him the way; and setting outposts, he assembled his men, and spoke to them.

"Soldiers," he said, "the Arcadians, or what is left of them, are besieged on a hill, and many have been killed. I think that if they are to be destroyed there will be no safety for us, with such hosts of enemies, so many and so bold. Then it is best for us to rescue these men, and have them fighting with us if they are still safe; or we shall be left alone and in danger. For there is no refuge for us here; it is a long way back to Heracleia, and a long way on to Chrysopolis, but the enemy are close by: the shortest way is to Calpe's Haven, where we suppose Cheirisophos to be, if he is safe.

"But then, you may think, no ships are there to sail in, and if we stay there, not even one day's provisions. But if the besieged men are lost, it is a greater danger for us to have only Cheirisophos with us than if they are saved, all together to hold on to safety. Then we must make up our minds to do a noble feat in saving so many Hellenes, or to find a glorious end this day! It may be that God leads us now, whose will is to humble the boastful as over-proud, but to make us more honourable than they are, because we do nothing without asking first the grace of God.

"So you must follow, and let your one thought be to obey orders. Let us go forwards now until it seems to be time for supper; and while we are marching, let Timasion ride ahead with the horsemen, keeping us in sight, and let him explore in front that we may miss nothing."

Then he led the way. He sent scouts on the flanks and up the hills, active men from the light-armed troops, to signal if they saw signs of anything approaching, and he gave orders to set on fire all that would burn. The horsemen scattered as far as was convenient, the targeteers climbed the heights, and all set fire to whatever they saw that would burn, and so did the army if they found something left: so the whole country seemed to be in a blaze, and the army appeared very large. When the time came, they encamped off the road on a hill; they saw the enemy fires about five miles off, and they lit as many fires as possible themselves. As soon as they had supped, the order was given to quench the fires. Outposts were set, and they slept all that night.

But at daylight they offered prayer to the gods, and marched forward in battle order as quickly as they could. Timasion with the guides found themselves without knowing it on the hill where the Hellenes had been besieged. They saw no army, neither enemies nor friends, and reported this to Xenophon and his men; but there were a few old women and old men and sheep and cattle left behind. At first they wondered what had happened, but they learnt from those left behind that the Thracians had decamped after nightfall and were gone; and the Hellenes were gone, where they did not know.

Hearing this news, after breakfast, Xenophon and his party packed up and marched, hoping to meet the others at Calpe's Haven. On the march they saw the tracks of the Arcadians and Achaians on the road to Calpe; and when they reached the place, the two parties saw each other with joy and embraced like brothers. The Arcadians asked Xenophon's men why they had put out their fires. "When we saw no fires," they said, "at first we thought you would attack the enemy that night; and the enemy feared that, as it seemed to us, and went away for that reason; for they did go about that time. But as you never came, and it was too late, we thought you had learnt all about us and that frightened you, so you scampered away to the sea. Then we decided not to be left behind, and so we came here too."

IV

That day they spent under the open sky on the shore beside the harbour. The place called Calpe's Haven is in

Asiatic Thrace. This Thrace extends from the mouth of
the Euxine, along the sea to Heracleia on the right. In a
ship-of-war it is a long day's journey by oar to Heracleia
from Byzantion; in between there is no city either Hellenic
or friendly, but only the Thracians of Bithynia; any Hellenes
they take shipwrecked or otherwise they are said to treat
with great cruelty. Calpe's Haven lies half-way on the voyage
between Heracleia and Byzantion. It is a promontory jutting
out into the sea; the part by the sea being a sheer cliff, height
where it is least no less than twenty fathoms, and facing
the land a neck about four hundred feet wide. The space
inside the neck is enough for ten thousand inhabitants. The
harbour under the cliff has a beach towards the west. There
is a spring of plentiful sweet water close beside the sea commanded by the promontory. There is abundance of all sorts
of wood, and particularly a great deal of fine wood for
shipbuilding close to the sea. The highland stretches into
the country some two or three miles, good soil without
stones; and the part along the seashore is longer still, set
thick with much timber of all sorts. The rest of the country
for a long way round is good, and has many villages full
of people; the land bears barley and wheat and pulse of all
sorts, millet and sesame, figs enough, plenty of grapes, good
wine-grapes too, and everything else except olives. So much
for the country.

They encamped on the beach beside the sea. They would
not camp on a place which might be turned into a city,
and they thought indeed that they had really been brought
there by some scheme of persons who wanted to found a
city. For most of the soldiers had not been driven by poverty
to this expedition; but it was the fame of Cyros which had
brought them, some had followers with them, some had
spent money themselves, and a few others had run away
from home—they had left father and mother, or even children too, hoping to return with wealth for them, since they

had heard how others had made their fortunes with Cyros. Men such as these wished to return safe to Hellas.

On the next day after this meeting Xenophon made sacrifice for an expedition, since he must lead them out for provisions; he intended also to bury the dead. The omens were good; they set out, and the Arcadians went with them. Most of the dead they buried where they fell; it was already five days ago, and the bodies could not be removed; others who lay on the roads, however, they did collect, and buried them with all possible ceremony. For those they could not find they made a great cenotaph, and laid garlands upon it, and then returned to camp.

That evening they supped and slept there. On the next day there was a general meeting of the soldiers, summoned chiefly by Agasias the Stymphalian, captain, and Hieronymos the Elean, captain, and certain others, the seniors of the Arcadians. They passed a resolution, that for the future if anyone proposed to divide their army he should be punished with death; and now that the army should resume the arrangement they had before, and the former captains be in command. Cheirisophos was dead already, from some medicine he took in his fever. Neon of Asine took his place.

After this Xenophon rose and spoke. "Soldiers," he said, "it is clear that our journey must be made by land, for we have no ships; and it is necessary to march at once, for if we stay we have no food. Then we," says he, "will make sacrifice; and you must prepare yourselves to fight now if ever you did, for the enemy are full of confidence."

Then the captains sacrificed; they had a seer, Arexion the Arcadian, for Silanos the Ambraciot was gone before this; he had hired a ship at Heracleia and shown his heels. They sacrificed for departure, but the omens were not good, so they waited that day. Some persons made so bold as to say that Xenophon wanted to found a city there, and he had persuaded the seer to declare the omens unfavourable.

Then on the morrow he cried round the camp that the sacrifice was open to all comers, and invited any seer there might be to come and inspect the ceremony, and then sacrificed; great numbers were present. Sacrifice was made as many as three times, and the omens were unfavourable. Then the soldiers were very angry, for the provisions they had with them were nearly done, and there was no market yet.

After this they had a meeting, and Xenophon said, "Gentlemen, for our departure, as you see, the omens are not yet favourable; but I see you need provisions, and I think it necessary, then, to sacrifice about just that." Someone rose and said, "There is good reason why the omens are bad. I heard from someone on board a ship which came in yesterday by accident. Cleandros the governor of Byzantion intends to come with transports and ships-of-war!" Then they all decided to stay; but the provisions had to be got, and there must be some expedition. Again he sacrificed three times for this, and the omens were unfavourable. Men were already coming to Xenophon's tent and saying they had nothing to eat; but he refused to lead them out without good omens.

Again he wanted to sacrifice next day; and almost the whole army was crowded about the place, because all were concerned, but no victims were to be had. The captains did not lead them out, but summoned a meeting. So Xenophon said, "Perhaps the enemy are gathered and we shall have to fight. Then if we leave the baggage in the strong place up there and go out ready for battle, perhaps the omens might be good." The soldiers shouted out, "No need to take us to that place; sacrifice and look sharp!" Sheep still could not be found, but they brought an ox from under a cart and sacrificed; and Xenophon begged Cleanor the Arcadian to look after it, in case something was there. But even so there was nothing good.

Neon was captain in place of Cheirisophos, and when he saw the men in a miserable state from want, he wanted to do them a good turn. He found some fellow from Heracleia, who said he knew villages near where they could get their provisions, so he sent round a herald to cry, "If anyone wishes to go for provisions, follow me!" They came out then, with poles and skins and bags and bowls, two thousand of them. But when they were among the villages, and scattered to get what they could, Pharnabazos's cavalry fell on them first: they had come to support the Bithynians, wishing with the Bithynians to keep the Hellenes from entering Phrygia, if they could. These horsemen killed no fewer than five hundred of the men; the rest escaped to the highlands.

One of those who escaped brought the news to the camp. Since the other sacrifices that day had been unfavourable, Xenophon took a bullock from a cart (there were no other victims) and cut its throat, and went to the rescue with all up to thirty years of age. They picked up the rest of the party and brought them back to camp. It was already about sunset, and the Hellenes were supping, very miserable, when suddenly out of the brakes some Bithynians attacked the outposts, and killed some, and drove the rest into the camp. Shouts and cries brought all the Hellenes running for their arms; but to pursue, and to move the camp at night, was thought to be not safe, for the place was covered with bush. They spent the night under arms, with sufficient outposts to keep watch.

v

So they spent the night; and at daybreak the captains led them to the strong place. They followed with arms and baggage. Before the time of breakfast, they dug a ditch across the entry into the stronghold, and fenced all in with stakes, leaving three gates. A ship arrived from Heracleia,

bringing barley-meal and wine and sacrificial victims. Xenophon rose early, and sacrificed for an expedition, and had
good omens in the first victim. And just at the end of the
sacrifice, the seer Arexion the Parrhasian spied an eagle,
and told Xenophon to lead on.

They crossed the trench and grounded arms, and sent
round a herald with orders that the men should breakfast
and then come out under arms; the mob and the captives
to be left there. All came except Neon, for it seemed best
to leave him on guard in the camp; but his officers and men
began to desert him, being ashamed not to follow when
the others went out, and all over forty-five years of age in
the army were sent back to him. These remained, then, and
the rest marched out. Before they had gone two miles they
came on dead bodies; and when they brought up the rear
of their division level with the first bodies found, they
buried all covered by the division. Having buried the first
ones, they pushed on until the rear was level with the first
of the unburied, and then buried in the same way all that
the army covered. But when they reached the road from the
villages, where they lay in heaps, they collected them and
buried them together.

It was now past midday; they still led the army forward
but outside the villages, and seized all they set eyes on within
the line, when suddenly they beheld the enemy coming over
the crest of some hills opposite, and marshalled in line of
battle, large numbers of horse and foot; for Spithridates
and Rhathines were there from Pharnabazos with their
forces. When the enemy caught sight of the Hellenes they
halted about two miles off. At once Arexion the Hellenic seer
sacrificed, and in the very first victim the omens were good.
Then Xenophon said, "I propose, gentlemen, to appoint
reserve companies for the line, so that in case of need there
will be troops to support, and when the enemy are in some
disorder they may meet opponents in good order and fresh."

All approved this. "Advance, then," said he, "straight on our foes. Don't let us stand still, now we have seen them and they have seen us. I will detach the last companies, as you have approved, and come on."

After this the main body advanced quietly, and he detached the three rear sections, two hundred men each. He sent one to the right, ordering it to follow at a distance of a hundred feet: Samolas the Achaian was in command of this section. The second he placed in the centre; Pyrrhias the Arcadian was in command here. The other one he placed on the left, in command of Phrasias the Athenian.

On the way the leading party came to a ravine, a deep, difficult place, and they stood doubtful whether they should cross it. Word was sent back calling officers and captains to the front. Xenophon wondered what the check could be, and soon hearing the summons he rode forward at full speed. When they met, Sophainetos the senior captain said the question was not worth discussing, whether they ought to cross a ravine like that. Xenophon broke in firmly and said:

"You know, gentlemen, that I have never urged you to any danger if I had the choice. You need no reputation for courage, as I can see; it's life or death now! Without fighting we cannot get out of this; if we do not attack, the enemy will follow whenever we retreat, and fall on us. Think, then, whether it is better to go for the enemy with arms in front, or reverse arms and watch him following behind! You know, moreover, that to retreat before the enemy is not for a man of honour, but to attack makes even a coward bold. I would rather myself attack with half this number than retreat with double the number!

"As for these men—I know you expect yourselves that they will not stand before us, but if we retreat we all know they will dare to follow. And to cross, leaving a difficult ravine behind us, when we are going to fight, is surely an advantage worth taking! For the enemy, I should like to give every opportunity to retreat; for us, the ground itself ought to teach us that only victory can give safety. I'm really surprised if anyone thinks this ravine more terrible than the other places we have passed. How can that plain be passed if we do not beat the cavalry? Or the mountains which we have passed, if all those light troops are following? And suppose we do get safe to the sea, what a huge ravine is the Euxine! No ships are there to carry us, no food if we stay there, and no sooner shall we be there than we shall have to sally in search of provisions! Surely it is better to fight now to-day after a good breakfast than to-morrow after none at all! Men, the victims are favourable, the omens are good, the sacrifice excellent—let us go for them! Now they have seen us at all, these men must not be left to dine comfortably and camp where they will!"

Then the captains told him to lead on, and no-one objected. So he led on, giving orders for each man to cross where he found himself; he thought the army would get over more quickly all together, than filing by the bridge like a skein of wool where it spanned the valley. As soon as they had crossed he went along the line and spoke to them:

"Men," he said, "remember how many battles you have won, with God's help, by coming to handgrips! Remember what happens to those who run before their foes! Do not forget that we stand at the door of Hellas. Follow Leader Heracles and cheer on each other by name. What a delight now to say and do something honourable and brave, and to leave such a memory of ourselves with those whom we wish to remember us!"

So he exhorted them, riding along, and he began to lead them himself in line of battle. They posted the targeteers on each flank, and marched for the enemy. The order was to hold spears on the right shoulder until the trumpet sounded, then drop them to the charge and march forward steadily, no-one to double. Then the watchword went round, Zeus Saviour, Heracles Leader!

The enemy stood their ground, thinking they had a good position. When the Hellenes were close up, with a cheer the targeteers doubled to the attack without orders; the enemy came out to meet them, both cavalry and a mass of Bithynians, and drove back the light troops. But when the line of heavy-armed men came up marching fast the trumpet sounded at once, they chanted their hymn, and cheered Eleleu! and at once down came the spears: then the enemy stood no longer but broke into flight. Timasion with his horsemen gave chase, and killed all they could, a few men like that.

The enemy left wing was dispersed at once, where the Hellenic horsemen were; but the right wing, being not vigorously pursued, rallied upon a hill. As soon as the Hellenes saw them making a stand they thought the easiest and safest thing was to charge them, and charge they did, chanting the battle-hymn. Then they stood no longer; the targeteers pursued until the right wing was scattered, but few were killed, for the enemy cavalry was formidable, being a large body.

The Hellenes could see the horse of Pharnabazos in formation still, and the Bithynian horse rallying to these, and watching the scene from a hill; tired as they were, they determined to attack them as best they could, and not to let them recover their spirits and rest.

So they formed up and marched. Then the enemy horse took flight down the steep just as if cavalry were pursuing. A valley received them which the Hellenes had not noticed, and they gave up the pursuit, for it was late. So they returned to the place where the first encounter had been; and putting up a trophy, they set out for the sea about sunset: it was about seven miles to the camp.

VI

After this the enemy kept to themselves, and brought away the inhabitants and their goods as far as possible; but the Hellenes waited for Cleandros and the transports and ships of war which they expected. Each day they sallied out with animals and slaves, and brought in plenty of wheat and barley, wine, vegetables, millet, and figs, for the country had all good things except olive oil. When the army remained to rest anyone had leave to raid for booty, and those who raided kept what they got; but whenever the army went on some expedition together, if any one got private spoil it was put in the common stock. Now there was plenty of everything; markets were provided from all sides by the Hellenic cities, and ships coasting by gladly put in, hearing there was a city with people in it and a harbour. The enemy also thereabouts sent to Xenophon, hearing that he was making a city in the place, to ask what they could do to be friends. He referred them to the soldiers.

Meanwhile Cleandros arrived, with two ships-of-war but no transports, to find the camp empty, the main body of the army being away. Some of the troops had gone into the hills foraging and captured a number of sheep; they were afraid that these might be taken away, and told Dexippos, the man who had shown a clean pair of heels from Trapezûs with the fifty-oar galley. They said he might take some if he left them the rest. At once he drove off the soldiers standing round and saying they were public property; Dexippos informed Cleandros that this was an attempt at robbery. Cleandros told him to bring the robber, and he caught someone and brought him. Agasias met him and rescued the man, who belonged to his company. The other soldiers there began to pelt stones at Dexippos, calling out "Traitor!" Many of the naval men ran off to the sea in fear, and Cleandros ran too.

Xenophon and the captains put a stop to this, and told Cleandros that there was nothing in it, the general rule in the army was the reason. But Cleandros allowed himself to be goaded on by Dexippos, and he was angry too for having been frightened; he said he would sail away, and declare them public enemies, and forbid all cities to receive them. At that time the Lacedaimonians were the leading state in Hellas.

The matter began to look ugly, and the Hellenes begged him not to do so. He said he was resolved unless they delivered over to him the robber and the man who began stoning. Agasias was one of the men he demanded, and he was always Xenophon's friend; that was why Dexippos denounced him.

In this difficulty the commanders called all to a meeting. Some of them made light of Cleandros; but Xenophon did not think it a trifling matter, and he rose and spoke.

"Soldiers and gentlemen, I think it no trifling matter if Cleandros is to leave us with this intention as he declares. The Hellenic cities are close at hand, and the Lacedaimonians are at the head of Hellas. They are able, and any one of them is able, to arrange what they will in the cities. If he first closes Byzantion against us, and then forbids the other governors to receive us, as public enemies to Lacedaimon and lawless men, and if this reputation comes to Admiral Anaxibios, it will be difficult either to go or to stay: on land the Lacedaimonians are masters, and so they are at sea now. Then we must not shut all of us out of Hellas for the sake of one man, or two; no, we must obey whatever they command, for even the cities we come from obey them. I take it on myself, then; for I hear Dexippos has told Clearchos that Agasias would never have done this unless I had commanded him. I clear you all, then, from the charge, and Agasias too, if Agasias himself says I am to blame; and I condemn myself, if I am the inciter of stoning or any other violence, to be worthy of the extreme penalty, and I will face the penalty. I say also that if he accuses anyone else, he must give himself up to Cleandros for judgment; thus you will all be free of the charge. But as things are now it is hard if we are to be thought not even equal to others, instead of winning praise and honour in Hellas, and if we are to be excluded from all Hellenic cities."

After this Agasias rose and spoke.

"I take my oath, gentlemen, by all gods and goddesses, that Xenophon did not command me to rescue the man, and no-one else did command me. I saw an honest man of my company being dragged away by Dexippos, one who was traitor to you as you know, and I thought it a shame and rescued him, I admit. You need not surrender me; I will surrender myself, as Xenophon says, to Cleandros, that he may judge me as he shall please. Don't make war on Lacedaimonians for that, but go safely with your lives where each one shall wish. However, elect some of yourselves and send them with me to Cleandros, to speak and act on my behalf if I omit anything."

Then the army left it to him to choose any he wished, and he chose the captains. After this they went before Cleandros, Agasias and the captains and the man whom Agasias had rescued. The captains spoke and said:

"We have been sent by the army to you, Cleandros. If you accuse all, they ask you to be judge yourself and do to us all what you think best; or if you accuse one, or two, or more, they expect these to surrender themselves to you for judgment. Then if you accuse any of us in any point, we are here before you; if anyone else, tell us who; no-one shall be absent who will obey us."

Next Agasias stept forward: "I am the man, Cleandros," he said, "who rescued that man from the hands of Dexippos, and gave the order to strike Dexippos. For the man, I know, is an honest man; and Dexippos, I know, was elected by the army to command that fifty-oar galley which we borrowed from the Trapezuntians to collect transports for our rescue, and I know Dexippos absconded and betrayed the soldiers with whose help he had been saved alive: so we robbed Trapezûs of the fifty-oar galley and we got a bad name on his account, and he has destroyed us as far as his own part goes. For he heard, as we did, that it was impossible for us to march by land and cross those rivers and come home safe to Hellas. Such is the man whom I robbed of his prey. If you had seized him, or any from you, not a deserter from ourselves, I assure you that I would have done none of these things. Then if you put me to death now, be assured that you are executing an honest man for a coward and a criminal."

Cleandros heard them, and said that he could not commend Dexippos if he had done that; but he did not consider that violence ought to be offered to Dexippos, however bad he might be. "He ought to be tried and judged," he said, "as you claim yourselves, before punishment. Then leave this man with me now, and go; and when I command you, present yourselves at the judgment. I accuse neither the army nor anyone else further, now that this man himself admits that he rescued the man." The rescued man said, "Let me speak, sir, for myself; if you think I had done any wrong that I should be arrested, I struck no-one, I cast no stone, I only said the sheep were public property; for it was a general rule in the army that when the army was raiding, if anyone got private spoil, what he took was public property. That is all I said; and immediately this man arrested me and began to hale me off; in order that no-one might utter a word, but he might take some for himself and keep the rest for the robbers contrary to the rule." Cleandros answered, "Then you stay too, since you say that, and we will consider your case also."

After this, Cleandros and his people had breakfast, and

Xenophon summoned the army to meet, and advised them
to send a deputation to Cleandros and ask mercy for the
men. Accordingly it was decided to send captains and officers, with Dracontios the Spartan noble, and others who
seemed appropriate, and petition Cleandros to release the
two men. So Xenophon came before him, and said:

"Now, Cleandros, you have the men; the army has
yielded to your will, both in this and in all else. Now they
beg and pray you to give up the two men and not to put
them to death; for they have served the army well in time
past. If you grant this, they promise for the future, if you
will lead them and if the gods are gracious, to show you
how orderly they are, and how well fitted to fear no enemy,
with heaven's help, while they obey their commander. They
pray this also, that you will come and take command of
them, test them and Dexippos too, and find out what each is
like, and then give each man his due."

Cleandros listened, and said, "Now be the twa gads,[1] "
says he, "I'll soon answer you that. Take the two men as a
gift, and I will come too, and if God grants it I will lead
you all home to Hellas. This is a very different tale from
what I heard from some people, that your whole army was
apostate from the Lacedaimonians."

Then they thanked him and went away with the two
men. Cleandros made sacrifice for the journey, and was
most cordial with Xenophon, and they struck up a friendship together. When he saw them obeying orders punctili-
ously, he wished more than ever to be their leader. However, after he sacrificed on three days and found no good
omens, he summoned the captains, and said, "I can't get
omens for myself to take you away, but don't lose heart on
account of that. You, it seems, are decreed to be the leaders;
then go ahead. And when you come to your journey's end,
we will entertain you as handsomely as we can."

Upon this they resolved to give over the public sheep to

[1] The Spartan oath, by Castor and Polydeuces. In the Spartan dialect.

him, and he gave them back. Then he set sail; and the soldiers divided up the corn they had collected, and their other spoils, and set out through the Bithynian country.

They followed the main road for some time; but finding no means of putting something in their pockets before they came into a friendly land, they turned right about and marched for a day and a night in the opposite direction. By doing this they captured many slaves and much cattle, and in six days they reached Chrysopolis in Calchedonia, and there they stayed seven days selling their spoil.

BOOK SEVEN

ͰͰ

I

After this Pharnabazos was afraid that the army might march into his country; so he sent to Admiral Anaxibios, who was in Byzantion as it happened, and begged him to transport the army out of Asia, promising to do all that was necessary. Anaxibios summoned the captains and officers to Byzantion, and promised service and pay for the soldiers if they would cross. Most of them said they would discuss it and return an answer, but Xenophon replied to him that he wished to leave the army at once and sail. Anaxibios asked him to wait and cross with the rest, and he said he would.

Now Seuthes the Thracian sent Medodases to Xenophon, and asked him to do his best to get the army across, and said if he did he should not be sorry for it. Xenophon replied, "The army will cross in any case; for that, let him pay nothing to me or to anyone. But as soon as it has gone across, I shall take my leave; let him deal as far as he thinks safe with those who remain and appear most important."

Soon all the soldiers had crossed over to Byzantion. Anaxibios did not find pay for the men, but made proclamation that all were to take their arms and baggage and go, as if all he wanted was to count them and give them a send-off. Then the soldiers were indignant, because they had not money to pay for their food on the way, and they took their time about packing. But Xenophon went to pay a parting visit to Cleandros the governor, with whom he had made friendship as has been described; and he said, "Don't go now, or else," says he, "you will be blamed. Even now some find fault with you because the army will not clear out quickly." He answered, "I can't help that. The men themselves want money to pay for their keep, and that's why they are so slack about going." "All the same," says he, "I advise you to leave as if you meant to go, and as soon as the army is outside get away from them." "Well, then," said Xenophon, "let's go and arrange that with Anaxibios."

So they went and told him. He said that was what they should do; let them pack up and march out by the quickest road, and he added that whoever was not present at the review must take the consequences.

Then out they went, the captains first and the others after; it was a clean sweep of all but a few; and Eteonicos stood by the gates, to close the gates and fix the bar as soon as all were outside. Anaxibios summoned captains and officers, and said, "Provisions," says he, "you will find in the Thracian villages; there is plenty of barley and wheat there, and everything else. Take it and march to the Chersonese, and there Cyniscos will give you pay." Some of the men heard this, or else one of the captains informed the army. The captains inquired about Seuthes, whether he was friend or enemy, and whether they must go by the Holy Mountain of Athos, or round through the middle of Thrace.

While they were talking, some of the men caught up their arms and set off at a run for the gates, intending to get within the walls again. Eteonicos and his party saw the heavy troops running for the gates, and closed them at once and threw in the bar. The men began battering the gates, and called out it was a shame to throw them out amongst the enemy; said they would smash the gates unless they would open them from inside. Others rushed down to the sea, and climbed by the breakwater over the wall into the city; others of the soldiers who were within, seeing this business at the gates, cut the bars with their axes and flung the gates open, and in they all came.

Xenophon saw all this; and fearing that the army might turn to pillage, and incurable trouble might follow for the city and for himself and the soldiers, ran and got through the gates along with the mob. When the townspeople saw the army breaking in, they fled from the market, some home, some to boats and ships; all that happened to be indoors ran out, some launched the ships-of-war, hoping for safety in them, and all believed themselves to be lost as if the city had been taken by storm.

Eteonicos took refuge in the citadel. Anaxibios ran down to the sea, and sailed round in a fishing-boat to the acropolis, and at once sent across for the garrison from Calchedon, since the men in the acropolis did not seem strong enough to keep them off.

When the soldiers caught sight of Xenophon, a number threw themselves upon him, crying out, "Now be a man, Xenophon! Now's your chance! You have a city, you have ships-of-war, you have money, you have all these men! Now, if you wish, you can help us, and we can make you great!" He answered, "Well said, I'll do it. If that is what you want, ground arms and form up at once." He wished to quiet them, so he passed the word along himself, and told them to pass it on to the others, Ground arms. They arranged themselves in order; the heavy-armed were formed eight deep in a short time, and the light-armed ran to each wing. The place is excellent for drill, what is called the Thracian Square, being open and bare of houses. When the arms were grounded and they were quiet, Xenophon called them to meeting and spoke.

"You are angry," said he, "soldiers and gentlemen, and you think it a great shame to be deceived; and I am not surprised. But if you indulge your tempers, and punish these Lacedaimonians here for the deceit, and sack the city which is not to blame, think what will be the result. We shall be proved enemies to the Lacedaimonians and their allies. What the war will be like you may guess, when you remember recent events which you have seen.

"We Athenians began war against the Lacedaimonians and their allies when we had fleets at sea or in the dockyards of not less than three hundred ships, when we had great store of wealth in the city, and yearly income from our own people and from foreign parts of not less than one thousand talents. We had command of all the islands, we held many cities in Asia and others in Europe, including this very Byzantion where we now are. All this we had, and fought the war, with the result which you all know. Then what do we expect to happen now, when the Lacedaimonians have all their old allies, and they have added the Athenians and all who then were their allies too, when Tissaphernes and the other barbarians on the sea are all our enemies; and bitterest enemy of all the Great King up country, whom we came to kill and deprive of his empire if we could! With all these combined together, is any of you so foolish as to think we can prevail? Don't let us be mad, in God's name! Don't let us perish dishonourably, the enemies of our own countries, yes, and our friends and relations! They are all in those cities which will fight against us. And they will be right to do so, when we refused to hold one barbarian city when we had the power, if we are to sack the first Hellenic city we reach!

"Indeed I pray to heaven that I may lie ten thousand

fathoms underground before I see you doing that! I advise you as Hellenes to try to get your just rights while still in obedience to the rulers of the Hellenes. If you fail in this we must bear our wrongs, but never shut ourselves out of Hellas. Now, then, I think it is our duty to send a deputation to Anaxibios, and tell him that we have come back into the city not meaning to do violence of any sort but hoping to be relieved a little by them; we will make it plain, however, that we go, not deceived, but obedient."

This was agreed; and they sent with this message Hieronymos the Elean and Eurylochos the Arcadian and Philesios the Achaian. The men went with their message.

While the soldiers were still in session, a certain Coiratadas arrived; he was a Theban on his travels, not a banished man but one with a fever for generaleering, ready with his services if army, city, or nation wanted a good commander. He came and said he was ready to lead them to what is called the Delta of Thrace, where they could get all sorts of good things; until they got there, he would find plenty of food and drink. While he was speaking, the answer came from Anaxibios: that if they were obedient they should never be sorry for it; he would report it to the authorities at home, and he would himself do all he could for them. Accordingly, the soldiers accepted Coiratadas for their general, and went outside the walls. Coiratadas arranged to be there the next day with victims for sacrifice, and a seer, and food and drink for the army. When they were outside, Anaxibios closed the gates and proclaimed that any soldier caught inside would be sold as a slave.

Next day Coiratadas appeared with his victims and seer, followed by twenty men bringing barley meal and twenty more with wine, three with olives, and one with the biggest load of garlic he could carry, and another with onions. He dumped these down for distribution, and went on with the sacrifice.

Xenophon sent for Cleandros, and asked him to manage how he might come within the walls and sail from Byzantion. Cleandros came and said, "What a job I had to arrange it! Anaxibios says it is not convenient; that the soldiers are close by the walls, and Xenophon inside; the Byzantines are all factions quarrelling with each other; however, he says you may come in if you are to sail with him." Accordingly Xenophon said goodbye to the soldiers, and went in with Cleandros.

But Coiratadas on the first day had no good omens, and gave nothing to the soldiers. On the second day the victims were standing by the altar and Coiratadas with a garland on ready to sacrifice, when up came Timasion the Dardanian and Neon the Asinonian and Cleanor the Archomenian, and told Coiratadas not to sacrifice, for he should not be their general unless he would give them something to eat. "All right," he said, "dole out." But finding that there was not nearly enough for a day's food all round, he picked up his victims and departed. He said he did not care to be general.

II

Neon of Asine and the Achaians Phryniscos and Philesios and Xanthicles, and Timasion the Dardanian, remained in charge of the army, and they encamped among the villages near Byzantion. Then the captains quarrelled. Cleanor and Phryniscos wanted to march to Seuthes,[1] who had persuaded them by giving a horse to one and a woman to the other. Neon voted for the Chersonese, believing that if they came under Lacedaimonians, he would be put at the head of the whole army. Timasion was eager to go over to Asia again, hoping to return home; the soldiers wanted the same. Time was wasted, and many of the soldiers dispersed, some selling their arms here or there and taking ship where they could, some joining the cities. Anaxibios was glad to

[1] a Thracian king

hear all this, how the army was dwindling; that's the best way to please Pharnabazos, he thought.

Anaxibios on his voyage from Byzantion was met in Cyzicos by Aristarchos, who was to succeed Cleandros as governor of Byzantion; it was said also that his own successor, Polos, was all but in the Hellespont by this time. Anaxibios instructed Aristarchos to sell as slaves any of Cyros's men he might find left; but Cleandros sold none, he even cared for the sick and made people take them in. But Aristarchos, when he came, did sell as many as four hundred. Anaxibios, coming to Parion in his voyage, sent a message to Pharnabazos as had been arranged. However, Pharnabazos cared nothing for Anaxibios, when he was no longer admiral; but as soon as he learnt that Aristarchos had arrived at Byzantion to be governor, he made the same arrangements with him about Cyros's army as he had made with Anaxibios.

Consequently Anaxibios called Xenophon, and begged him by every manner of means to sail with all haste to the army, to gather and hold together as many of the scattered men as he possibly could, to bring them down to Perinthos and across into Asia with all speed; he gave him a fifty-oar galley and a letter, and sent a man with him to order the Perinthinas to supply Xenophon with horses and to escort him as far as the army. Xenophon sailed over and reached the army; the soldiers received him with delight and followed him gladly, ready to cross from Thrace into Asia.

Seuthes heard of this, and again sent Medosades to him by sea, and begged him to lead the army to himself, promising him what he thought would persuade him; but he answered that none of these things could be done. The messenger departed. When the Hellenes arrived at Perinthos, Neon broke away and encamped apart about with eight hundred men; all the rest of the army was in one place beside the walls of Perinthos.

Next Xenophon began to arrange for vessels to transport them across with all speed. Meanwhile Aristarchos arrived, the governor of Byzantion, with two ships-of-war (Pharnabazos was at the bottom of this). He forbade the skippers to take them aboard; and he came to the army and forbade the soldiers to cross into Asia. Xenophon said, "These are orders from Anaxibios, and he sent me here for this." Aristarchos again said, "Well, Anaxibios is no longer admiral, and I am governor here. If I catch any of you at sea, I will sink you." With these words he went back to his walls.

Next day he sent for the captains and officers of the army. When they were already close to the walls someone reported to Xenophon that if he entered he would be seized, and either do what he was told or be handed over to Pharnabazos. On hearing this he let the others go on and told them he wanted to make a sacrifice about something. He left them and sacrificed, asking if the gods would allow him to try to get away to Seuthes with the army; for he saw that it was not safe to cross when there were ships-of-war to prevent him, and he did not wish to be shut up in the Chersonese and let the army be destitute in a place where it was necessary to obey the governor, and the army would have no provisions.

Meanwhile the captains and officers had come back from Aristarchos, and reported that he bade them go away then and return later in the afternoon. Then it seemed clearer that there was a plot. Xenophon found the omens good for a safe journey to Seuthes; and therefore he took Polycrates the Athenian, and one trusty man from each of the captains except Neon, and travelled by night to the army of Seuthes, about eight miles.

As they drew near they came upon deserted watch fires. At first he thought Seuthes had gone somewhere else; but hearing a noise, and signallers calling to each other among his people, he understood what had happened; Seuthes had

lit the fires in front of his pickets, that any who came might
be seen clearly in the light, while the pickets would be in
the dark behind, and no-one could see how many they were,
or where. Accordingly he sent forward the interpreter he
had, with instructions to tell Seuthes that Xenophon wished
to meet him. They asked, "The Athenian from the army?"
He said, "That's the man," and they leapt up and off they
went; a little while after appeared targeteers, about two
hundred, who took charge of Xenophon and his men and
brought them to Seuthes.

He was in a tower strongly guarded, horses all round it
bridled and bitted. He was so much on the alert that he
gave them fodder in the daytime, when they might have
been grazing, and at night kept them in bit and bridle on
guard. For the story was that Teres, his ancestor in this
country with a large army, had been attacked by these people, and lost many men and all his baggage; they were the
Thynians, of all the world said to be most dangerous by
night in time of war.

When they were near he asked Xenophon to enter with
any two men he might choose. They entered, and first
greeted each other with toasts, and horns of wine in Thracian
fashion; beside Seuthes was Medosades, who went everywhere as his minister. Then Xenophon began by saying,
"You sent to me more than once, Seuthes. First, you sent
Medosades, who is present here, to Calchedon, asking me
to do my best to help in bringing over the army from Asia,
and you promised to make it worth my while if I could, so
Medosades here said." Then he asked Medosades if that
was true, and he said Yes. "A second time this same Medosades came, after I came over again to the army from Parion,
promising that if I brought the army to you, you would
treat me as your friend, and in particular that I should receive from you the places on the sea which you have in
your power." Then he asked Medosades again whether this

was true, and he said Yes, it was. "Then," said Xenophon, "repeat to him what I answered, first at Calchedon." "You answered that the army would cross to Byzantion in any case, and for that he need not pay anything to you or anyone else. You said you meant to sail away as soon as you yourself had crossed; and everything went as you said." "Well, then," said Xenophon, "what did I say when you came to Selymbria?" "You said it couldn't be done; they were going to Perinthos and meant to cross into Asia." "Well, then," said Xenophon, "at this moment I am here myself, and here is Phryniscos, one of the captains, and here is Polycrates, one of the other officers, and outside are others, one from each of the captains except Neon the Laconian, their most trusted men. So if you wish the transaction to be more strongly confirmed—go outside, Polycrates, and tell them to leave their arms there, and you leave your sword before you come back."

When Seuthes heard this he said that he would never distrust an Athenian; he knew they were his kinsmen, and believed them to be honest friends.[1] After this the men came in, and Xenophon first asked Seuthes how he wished to use the army. He answered:

"Maisades was my father, and his rule was over the Melanditans and Thynians and Tranipsans. Afterwards the Odrysians were in a bad way; my father was driven out, and died of disease, and I was brought up an orphan in the house of Medocos, the present king. When I grew up to be a young man I could not endure to live gazing at another's table, so I sat on the seat beside him, as a suppliant; I prayed him to give me as many men as he could, and let me try to revenge myself on those who threw us out, and not live gazing at another's table. Then he gave me the men, and the horses which you will see when daylight comes. And now I live by these, robbing my own ancestral country. But if you join me, I think I shall easily

---

[1] Legend connected Teres with the story of Tereus and Procne; see Aristophanes, *Birds,* 368 etc.

get back my dominions, please God. That is what I want of you."

"Very well," said Xenophon. "What could you give the army and its officers and captains? Speak, and let them report." He promised for each man a cyzicene, for each lieutenant two, and for each captain four, and as much land as they wish, yokes of oxen, and a fort on the sea.

"But," said Xenophon, "suppose we try and don't succeed, and there is a scare from the Lacedaimonians: will you receive them into your country, if anyone wishes to come?" He said, "That I will, and make them brothers, who shall sit on the same seat with me and share all we are able to get. And you, Xenophon! I will give you my daughter, and if you have a daughter I will buy her by Thracian law, and I will give you Bisanthe [1] to live in, the best fort I have on the sea!"

III

After this interview they exchanged pledges of faith and departed. Before daylight they were back at the camp, and all reported to those who had sent them. When day came Aristarchos summoned the captains, but they decided to ignore the summons and call a meeting. All came except Neon's men; they were about a mile off. When the meeting had assembled Xenophon spoke and said:

"Men, to sail where we wished is impossible; Aristarchos and the ships-of-war bar the way. Thus it is not safe to take ship, and this man himself orders us to march into Chersonese by force through the Holy Mountain. If we can fight our way there, he declares that he will not sell you as in Byzantion, or deceive you again: you shall receive pay, and he will not leave you in want of provisions any longer as you are now. That is what he says. And Seuthes says that if you join him, he will treat you well.

"Now consider whether you prefer to sit and deliberate

[1] Rodosto, at the entrance to the Holy Mountain Athos

here, or go up for provisions first. My own opinion is that, since here we have no money to buy with—and without money they forbid us to take any—we should go up among the villages where might gives right to take, and get our provisions there; then listen to what one or another asks of you, and choose what you think best. All in favour of this hold up a hand!" All held up hands. "Then go and pack up," he said, "and, when the signal comes, follow your leader."

Then Xenophon led, and they followed. Neon and others from Aristarchos tried to persuade them to turn back, but they would not listen. After they had gone on three or four miles, they were met by Seuthes, and Xenophon seeing him asked him to ride in that as many as possible should hear what he proposed. As soon as he was near enough, Xenophon said:

"We are marching to find food for this army; then we will hear both you and the Laconian's men, and choose what we think best. So if you will lead us where plenty of provisions are to be found, we shall believe ourselves to be your guests."

Seuthes answered, "Oh, I know heaps of villages with plenty of provisions, just far enough away that you may be in time for a comfortable breakfast." "Lead on, then," said Xenophon.

They reached the villages later in the afternoon, and the soldiers assembled, and Seuthes spoke as follows:

"What I ask, men, is to take the field with me. I promise to pay to each man a cyzicene, and to officers the usual thing; besides this, I will reward all merit. You shall have food and drink as now by taking it from the country; but whatever is captured I claim for myself, that I may dispose of it and so find your pay. Whatever runs away and hides we are able to chase and catch; if anyone resists, we will try to subdue them with your help." Xenophon asked,

"How far from the sea will you expect the army to follow you?" He answered, "Nowhere more than seven days, mostly less."

Then it was open for all to speak; and many did speak, very much the same, that this was an excellent offer of Seuthes. For winter had come, and there was no voyage home if any wished; it was impossible to get through as friends if they had to pay for their keep, and to stay and be fed in a hostile country was safer with Seuthes than alone, in all this plenty. And if they received pay too, they counted that a godsend. Xenophon ended all by saying, "Is there anyone against? If so, let him speak. If not, I will put it to the vote." No-one opposed, he put the vote; and it was carried. He went straight to Seuthes, and told him they would take the field with him.

After this the men encamped in their companies; and Seuthes invited all officers to dinner, having a village near. At the doors, as they were going in to dinner, they found a man Heracleides of Maroneia.[1] He approached each guest who seemed likely to have some present for Seuthes. First he addressed some Parians, some who were there to arrange friendship with Medocos, King of the Odrysians, who had brought gifts for him and his queen; and he said that Medocos was a long way up country, twelve days from the sea, and Seuthes would be master on the coast now that he had this army. "So he is your neighbour, and most able to do you good or evil. Then if you are sensible, you will give him what you bring; it will be better for you than if you give it to Medocos who lives a long way off." That was how he tried to get round those. Next he came to Timasion the Dardanian, since he had heard that he had oriental cups and rugs; said it was the custom when invited to dinner with Seuthes that the guests made presents to him. "If he becomes great here, he is able to send you home or to make you rich here." So he went up to everyone and

[1] a Hellenic city in Thrace

pleaded. He tried Xenophon also, and said, "You come from a very great city, and you have a very great name with Seuthes. Perhaps you will expect to take forts in this country, as others of your people have done, and land too. It is worth your while, then, to honour Seuthes magnificently. I give this advice out of goodwill, for I know that the more you give him, the more you will get from him." Xenophon was perplexed, for he had brought nothing from Parion but a servant and journey-money.

When the company was assembled, the chiefs of the Thracians there, and the captains and officers of the Hellenes, and any embassy there might be from various places, they were seated in a circle. Then three-legged stools were brought in for all; these were piled high with meat, and large pasties of leavened bread skewered to the meat. Generally the tables were set opposite the guests. For the custom was—and Seuthes began doing it now; he picked up the loaves nearest him, and broke them into pieces, and threw to any he thought fit, and so with the meat, leaving only a taste for himself. The others did the same if the tables were near them. But a certain Arcadian named Arystas, a rare one to eat, would not thank you for thrownabouts; he picked up a three-quartern loaf and the meat and put it across his knees and ate away. They carried round horns of wine, and all had some; but when the butler came to Arystas with his horn, and Arystas saw that Xenophon had done, he called out, "There's your man; give it to him, he's free, but I haven't time yet." Seuthes heard the sounds, and asked the butler what he said; the butler knew Greek, and told him. Then there was laughter.

When the drinking was well on, a Thracian man came in with a white horse, and, taking a full horn, he said, "I drink your health, Seuthes, and I present you with this horse. When you are on his back, you will catch anyone you like to pursue, and in retreat you will fear no foe."

Another brought in a boy, and gave him with another "Here's health!" and a third with robes for his wife. Timasion drank a health, and offered a bowl of silver and a rug worth forty pounds. An Athenian, Gnesippos, rose and said, "It was a good old rule that if you have, you give to the king to show him honour, and if you have not, the king gives to you, and then I too," says he, "may have a gift to honour him!" Xenophon did not know what on earth to do, for as a guest of honour he was on the seat nearest Seuthes. Then Heracleides told the butler to hand him the horn; and Xenophon, who had had a few drinks, boldly took the horn, and said, "And I, Seuthes, give you myself and these my comrades to be your true friends, and not a man of them unwilling—all wishing to be your friends even more than I do! Here they are, asking for nothing, but offering themselves to work for you and to face danger for you willingly. With their help, please God, you shall win back the country of your fathers, and win more to boot, a great dominion, and many horses, many men and fair women. You will not need to take them as spoil, but these men themselves will bring them to you as gifts." Seuthes got up and drank with him, and sprinkled the last drops over him.

After this, men came in sounding the horns which they use for signals, and trumpeting tunes on trumpets made of raw hide, something like the music of Egyptian strings. Seuthes himself stood up and roared a war-cry, and jumped aside very nimbly as if he were dodging a shot. Then jesters came in.

When the sun was setting, the Hellenes rose and said it was time to set the watch and give the watchword. They asked Seuthes to direct that none of the Thracians was to enter their camp in the night; they said, "Our enemies are Thracians, and you are our friends." After they had gone, Seuthes rose too, looking as sober as you like. He went out, and called the captains aside to say, "Gentlemen, our enemies do not yet know our alliance; then if we attack them before they are on their guard, and before they can prepare any defence, we could make a fine sweep of captives and spoil." The captains agreed, and told him to lead on. He said, "Get ready and wait for me. I will come at the proper time and pick you up with your light troops, and then with the gods' help I will lead you." Then Xenophon said, "If we are to have a night march, consider if our custom is better. In daylight, that part of the army leads which may be most suitable for the country, heavy troops or light troops or cavalry; but at night our custom is for the slowest arm to lead—in this way the divisions are least pulled apart, and they don't slip away from each other without being seen. If sections are pulled apart they often fall foul of each other, and do much harm, or suffer harm ignorantly." Seuthes answered, "You are right, and I will follow your custom. You shall have guides from the oldest of my men, who know the country best, and I will come last with my horses; I shall be at the head soon enough, I think, if necessary." They gave Our Lady of Athens as watchword, because of their kinship. Then they went to rest.

About midnight Seuthes was there with his horsemen, armed in their corselets, and his targeteers with their weapons. He gave the guides, the men-at-arms led, the targeteers followed, the horse kept the rear. When daylight came, Seuthes rode to the front and praised the Hellenic custom. "Often," he said, "while marching at night, I and the horses have broken off from the foot; now here the day shows us all together as we should be! Now you must wait here and rest a bit, and I will go on and scout."

Then he rode away, taking a path through the mountains. Coming to a patch of snow, he looked round to see if there were any tracks of men going forwards or backwards; but the snow was untrodden, as he saw, and he soon came back, and said, "Men, it will be all right, if God will; we shall give the fellows a surprise! I will go first with the horse, and then if we see anyone he will not get away and alarm them. You follow me; if we get too far ahead, follow the horses' tracks. When we are over the mountains, we shall find plenty of prosperous villages."

By midday he was on the heights, and with a glance down at the villages he rode back to the heavy troops, and said, "Now I am going to send these down at a run, horsemen to the plain, targeteers to the villages. You come on at your best pace to support us if they resist."

Xenophon heard this, and got down from his horse; and Seuthes asked, "Why do you get down when speed is what we want?" Xenophon answered, "I know you don't want me alone; these men will run faster, and more contented, if I run at the head of them."

Then Seuthes was off, and Timasion went with him, and the Hellenic horsemen, about forty. Xenophon sent the word to each section, "All men of thirty and under, fall out!" Then he took all these active young fellows and went bowling along at the head of these, leaving the rest for Cleanor.

Arrived at the villages, Seuthes rode up with some twenty horsemen, and said, "It's just as you said, Xenophon, we have the fellows—but there are my cavalry gone off unsupported, chasing all over the place. I'm afraid the enemy will rally somewhere and do some mischief! Some of us must remain in the villages, for they are full of people." "I'll take the heights, then," said Xenophon, "with the men I have here; tell Cleanor to extend the line along by the villages." As soon as this was done, captives were collected, about a thousand, cattle two thousand, sheep and so forth ten thousand besides. Then they spent the night there in the open.

IV

Next day Seuthes burnt the villages completely, leaving not one house, to make the others afraid what would happen to them if they did not obey, and went back again. He sent Heracleides to Perinthos, in order to dispose of the spoil and find pay for the soldiers; he himself and the Hellenes encamped on the Thynian plain. The natives left it and took refuge in the highlands.

There was a great deal of snow and cold, so that the water they brought for supper froze, and the wine in the jars; and many of the Hellenes were frostbitten in nose and ears. Then it became clear why the Thracians wore the foxskin caps over head and ears, and shirts not only about the breast but over the thighs, and why they wear long wraps on horseback covering the feet, not merely cloaks.

Seuthes set free some of the captives, and sent them into the mountains to say that unless they would come down and live in their villages and obey him, he would burn their villages also, and their corn, and they should be starved to death. After this they came down, women and children and older men; the younger men were quartered in the villages under the mountains.

When Seuthes learnt this he told Xenophon to take the youngest of the heavy troops and follow him. They got up in the night, and by daylight they were at those villages. Most of the natives escaped, for the mountains were near; those he took Seuthes killed without mercy.

An Olynthian was there, Episthenes, a boylover; he saw a handsome boy, just old enough to bear a shield, about to be put to death, and running to Xenophon he begged him to save a handsome boy. Xenophon besought Seuthes not to kill the boy, and told him the ways of Episthenes; how he once enrolled a company, only careful they should be handsome boys, and then with these proved himself a good man. Seuthes asked him, "Would you be willing even to die for this boy, Episthenes?" The man stretched out his neck and said, "Strike! If the boy tells you, and if he will be grateful." Seuthes asked the boy if he should strike the man instead of himself. The boy said, "No, sir, don't kill either of us!" Thereupon Episthenes threw his arms round the boy and said, "Now then, Seuthes, fight me for the boy—I won't let him go!" Seuthes laughed, and said, "Oh, all right!"

But he decided to make bivouac there, that those in the mountains might get no food from the place. He went farther down into the plain himself and encamped there; and Xenophon with his picked men stayed in the highest village under the mountains, while the other Hellenes encamped near, among the people they call the Highland Thracians.

Not many days passed after this before the Thracians came down from the mountains, and treated with Seuthes for a truce and hostages. Xenophon also came to him, and said they were in bad quarters with the enemy close at hand; they would rather be quartered outside in strong places, than just under cover, plain destruction. Seuthes told him not to fear, and showed hostages there from them. And others came down to Xenophon from the mountains, and begged him to help them to make the truce. He agreed, and told them to fear nothing; he promised that no hurt should come to them if they obeyed Seuthes. But it turned out that they had come only to spy.

This was what happened in the day; but on the following night the Thynians came from the mountains and attacked him. They were led to each house by the master, for it was difficult otherwise to find the houses in those villages when it was dark, as the houses were fenced round with great stakes on account of the stock. When they came to the door of each house some threw in spears, others battered with their cudgels, which they carried to knock off the spearheads, as they said; others applied fire, and they called Xenophon by name to come out and die, or else they would burn him there. Fire was showing already through the roof, and Xenophon's men inside had their corselets on and shields and swords and helmets; then Silanos, a young Macistian of about eighteen, sounded the trumpet—and at once they leapt out sword in hand, and the men from the other places too.

The Thracians threw the light shields round to their backs, and ran, as their custom was. As they climbed over the palisade some of them were caught by their shields on the stakes and hung there; some missed the way and were killed; the Hellenes chased many of them out of the village. Some of the Thynians who had rallied in the dark cast javelins at the runners as they passed from darkness into the light beside a burning house; they wounded two captains, Hieronymos and Theogenes the Locrian, but killed no-one, although some lost clothes and baggage burnt.

Seuthes came to their aid with seven horsemen, the first he could find, and brought also his Thracian trumpeter. From the moment he heard of the trouble, and all the time he was coming, the horn was kept sounding, which struck terror into the enemy. When he arrived he clasped their hands, crying, "I thought I should find many dead."

After this Xenophon begged him to give him the hostages, and to join him in an expedition into the hills, or else to let him go alone. So next day Seuthes gave him the hostages, men well on in years, and, as they said, the most powerful of the highlanders; and he came himself with his force. The force was already thrice as large as before, since numbers of the Odrysians, hearing what he was about, had come down to join him. When the Thynians from the mountains saw so many men-at-arms, so many targeteers, so many horsemen, they came down and besought him to make peace, and promised to obey him and offered sureties. Seuthes called in Xenophon and explained what they said, and declared he would not make truce or peace if Xenophon wished to take revenge for the onslaught. He said:

"I think I have full satisfaction, if these are to be slaves instead of free men. However, I advise you in future to take as hostages those who can do the most mischief, and leave the old men at home."

Thus all in that part of the country submitted.

v

They now crossed over to the Thracians above Byzantion, into what is called the Delta; this was no longer the domain of Maisades, but of Teres the Odrysian. Heracleides was there already, with the price of the spoil. Seuthes then drove out three pairs of mules (there were only three, all the rest were oxen), called Xenophon and told him to take them, and to distribute the others among the officers. Xenophon said, "I can wait for another time; give these to those captains and officers who have served with me." So these pairs of mules went one to Timasion, one to Cleanor, one to Phryniscos; the pairs of oxen were distributed to the under-officers.

Then he gave the pay, but he could find pay only for twenty days, although the whole month was up. Heracleides declared that was all he had got for the sale. Xenophon was angry, and said with an oath, "I don't think you look after the interests of Seuthes as you should; if you had you would have brought the pay in full, even borrowing something if you couldn't help it, even selling your own clothes!"

Then Heracleides was angry, and feared he might lose the friendship of Seuthes; and he did all he could from that day to set Seuthes against Xenophon. Indeed, the soldiers blamed Xenophon because they had not their pay; Seuthes was angry with him because he dunned him for the pay.

So far he had been always saying that he would give him Bisanthe and Ganos and Newcastle, as soon as he got to the sea; but from that time he never mentioned them. For Heracleides kept dinning into his ears that it was not safe to give forts to a man who had an army.

Then Xenophon began to think what he was to do about the campaign up country. And Heracleides brought the other captains before Seuthes, and bade them say that they could lead the army quite as well as Xenophon; he promised them their pay within a few days, full pay for two months, and urged them to march. Then Timasion said:

"I would not go without Xenophon, not if you paid me for five months." Phryniscos and Cleanor agreed. Then Seuthes scolded Heracleides for not having brought Xenophon too.

Presently they invited him by himself. He understood the perfidy of Heracleides, and how he had been scheming against him with the captains; so when he came he brought the other captains and officers, and they all agreed.

So they set out together, and keeping the Euxine on the right, marched through the country of Millet-eating Thracians, as they are called, as far as Salmydessos. There many of the ships that sail into the Euxine run aground and are wrecked, for there are many shallows running out into the sea. The Thracians in those parts put up boundary marks, and plunder all that are cast into their portions; formerly, they say, many had been killed fighting with each other over the plunder, before they set up the marks. Here was a great find, beds and boxes and written books, and everything else which mariners carry in their wooden chests. Having reduced all this district, they came back.

By this time Seuthes had an army of his own larger than theirs; for many more had come down from the Odrysians, and his new subjects all joined with him. They made bivouac on the plain above Selymbria, three or four miles from the sea. No pay yet appeared; and the soldiers were very much put out with Xenophon, because he was no longer great with Seuthes, but if ever he wanted to see him many difficulties were put in the way.

VI

At this time, when nearly two months had passed, a mission came from Thimbron, Charminos the Laconian and Polyneicos. They said that the Lacedaimonians had resolved to make a campaign against Tissaphernes, and Thimbron had sailed for the war; that he wanted this army, and offered pay one daric per man per month, two for a lieutenant, and four for a captain.

As soon as these men arrived Heracleides heard they were visiting the army, and said to Seuthes, "Here's a great piece of luck! The Lacedaimonians want the army and you don't; then give them the army, and they won't ask for any more pay—they will just clear out of the country."

Seuthes, on hearing this, told him to bring the men in. They said they were visiting the army; and he said he would give it up, and wished to be their friend and ally, and invited them to a banquet, which was magnificent. But he did not invite Xenophon or any other of the captains. The Lacedaimonians asked, "What sort of a man is Xenophon?" "Not a bad sort," he said, "but too fond of his men. So much the worse for him!" "What," said they, "does he harangue the men?" Heracleides said, "I should think he does!" "Well, then," they said, "perhaps he will object to our carting them off?" "Just you collect them," said Heracleides, "and promise the pay; much they will care for him! Off they will run with you." "Then how could we get them together?" they wanted to know. "To-morrow," said Heracleides, "early in the morning we'll take you to them; and I am sure," says he, "as soon as they see you, they will run together glad enough." Thus ended that day.

Next morning the Laconians came to the army, led by Seuthes and Heracleides, and the men collected. Then two Laconians said, "The Lacedaimonians have resolved to make war on Tissaphernes, who has wronged you; then if you will go with us, you shall punish your enemy, and every man shall receive a daric per month, every lieutenant two darics, and every captain four."

The men were delighted to hear it. At once an Arcadian rose to accuse Xenophon. Seuthes was there also, wanting to hear what would be done, and stood with an interpreter within hearing; but he understood himself a good deal of Greek. Then the Arcadian said:

"We should have been with you long ago, Lacedaimonians, if Xenophon had not persuaded us and brought us here, and what a place! Through this dreadful winter we have been campaigning night and day without rest, and he enjoys our labours; Seuthes has made him a rich man privately, and he keeps our pay from us. If I could only see this man punished and stoned for dragging us about, I should call it pay in full, and I wouldn't worry about my labours." After this another got up and another, just the same, and at last Xenophon spoke:

"Then there is nothing a man must not expect in this world, as it seems, when I stand here now to be accused by you, and in something where I know in my conscience that I have used my utmost endeavours on your behalf. I was already on my way home, when I was turned aside by hearing of you—not because I heard you were in luck, not at all; no, I heard you were at your wits' end, and hoped to help you if I could. When I came to you, Seuthes, who is here present, sent messenger after messenger to me, and made great promises to me if I would persuade you to join him. Yet I did not try to do that, as you know yourselves; I led you to the place where I thought you could cross most quickly to Asia. I believed that to be best for you, and you

wished it, as I knew. Then Aristarchos came with ships
of war and stopt that.

"Next I did the natural thing, I suppose, and called you
together that we might consider what we must do. Aristarchos ordered you to go into the Chersonese. Seuthes tried
to persuade you to join his expedition: you heard both,
and all said go with Seuthes, all voted for that. What wrong
did I do you, then, when I led you where you all decided
to go? However, Seuthes deceived you about your pay: if
I praise him for that, you would have a right to hate me
and accuse me; if I am now wholly estranged from him,
having been formerly his especial friend, what right could
you have to blame me for this estrangement when I chose
you instead of Seuthes?

"Well, perhaps you might say that it is possible I got your
money from Seuthes, and I am just pretending. Then one
thing is clear: if Seuthes paid me anything, he did not expect
to have to pay it again to you, and so throw away what he
gave to me. Not so, I think; if he gave it, he would give
it on the understanding by paying me less he might avoid
paying you more. Very well, if you believe that happened,
you have the power here and now to make the transaction
worth less for both of us by demanding and getting the
money from him. It is clear that if I have had any of it
from him, he will ask for it back, and quite right too, if
I do not carry out the transaction for which I took the
bribe.

"Far from it—I have nothing of yours. I swear to you
solemnly by gods and goddesses all, that I have not even
what Seuthes promised me personally. He is present himself, and hears me, and knows whether I am forsworn.
What will surprise you more, I swear that I did not receive
even what the other captains did, no indeed, not even as
much as some of the under-officers. Why did I behave so?
I believed, gentlemen, that the better I helped him to bear

the poverty he had then, the better friend he would be when he should become powerful. But now I see him in his prosperity, and now I understand his mind.

"One might well ask whether I am not ashamed to be deceived like a fool. Upon my word, I should be ashamed indeed if an enemy had deceived me; but for a friend, I think it more disgraceful to deceive than to be deceived. If we can speak of precautions against a friend, I know we took every precaution to give him no just excuse not to pay what he promised; for we have done him no wrong, we never were slack, never dawdled over what he asked us to do.

"But, you might say, security ought to have been taken, that he might not have been able to deceive if he wished. Then listen to me while I tell what I should never have said in his presence, if you had not shown yourselves altogether stupid or else wholly ungrateful to me. Just remember what a state you were in when I brought you out to Seuthes. You went to Perinthos, but you couldn't get in— Aristarchos the Lacedaimonian shut the gates in your faces. You were outside in the open air, it was midwinter, you had a market, but there was little to buy and little to buy with; you were forced to remain in Thrace—for ships-of-war were there to prevent a crossing; but if you did remain, you would be in an enemy country; there were large forces of cavalry against you, and large forces of light troops, and what had we? A force of heavy-armed men, yes, and if we had taken it in a body to the villages perhaps we could have got some corn, nothing much; but to pursue and capture prisoners or sheep—we had nothing at all for that: I found no regular body at all of horse or targeteers with you. In such a necessity, if I had asked no pay at all from Seuthes and only got him for an ally, when he had the cavalry and light troops which you wanted, would you have thought I made a bad bargain for you? Only by sharing in those, of course, you found any amount of corn in the villages, because the Thracians were compelled to run away in a hurry, and you took more cattle and captives. Enemies —we never saw one of them any longer as soon as the horse was added to us; before that, the enemy followed us boldly with horse and light infantry, and we could not break into small bodies and scatter anywhere to get more abundant provisions. And if the man who provided this safety for you did not really give you very large pay for this safety, that is really dreadful treatment! And that's why you think I must never leave the place alive!

"And how are you off now? You are leaving this place; you have spent the winter in the midst of abundance, and whatever you got from Seuthes is so much to the good, for what you spent the enemy paid. Yes, and while this was your lot, you saw none of your comrades killed and you lost none alive. Besides, any fine feat you may have done against the barbarians in Asia, you have that safe and sound, haven't you? And now you have won a new glory by fighting the Thracians in Europe too and conquering them. I tell you that you ought to thank God for the very things you complain of, since they are blessings.

"So much for you; now be so kind as to consider my side of the question. When I set out for home that time I had your good wishes and best thanks, and through you I had a high reputation among all parts of our nation. I was trusted by the Lacedaimonians, or they would not have sent me back to you. I go now, reprobated by you before the Lacedaimonians, and disliked by Seuthes on your account, whom I hoped to serve along with you and to find in him an honourable refuge for myself and my children, if I should have any. And you, on whose behalf I have made many enemies and those more powerful men than I am, you for whom I have never ceased working and still work now to do you what good I can, that is your feeling for me.

Well, you have me. I did not avoid you, I did not run from you and let you catch me. If you do to me what you say, you will have slain a man who has spent many a sleepless night for you, who has shared many toils and dangers with you, in my turn and out of turn, one who when the gods were gracious has set up very many trophies of the barbarians by your side, and strained against you with all my strength to save you from becoming enemies to any of your countrymen. Indeed even now it is possible for you without reproach to travel where you please both by land and sea. But you, at the time when you have everything open to you, when you are sailing to the very place you have long desired, when great potentates want you and you can see your pay, when your leaders are the Lacedaimonians, by common consent the dominant power—this is exactly the time you think to be just right for putting me to death. But not in the time of our troubles: you have the best of memories, you never forget. No, then you called me father, and vowed always to speak of me as your benefactor. But these men who have come for you now are not hard-hearted themselves. As I take it, they will not think the better of you when you behave so to me." He spoke, and ceased.

Then Charminos the Lacedaimonian rose and spoke. He said:

"No, be the twa gads! I for one think you have no right to complain of this man. I'm a witness myself on his side. What Seuthes said when I and Polynicos asked about Xenophon, what sort of a man he was, what he said was he had only one fault to find; he said he was too fond of the soldiers, that's the reason why he didn't get on with us Lacedaimonians or with himself."

On this an Arcadian got up, Eurylochos of Lusia, and said to the two envoys, "My opinion is, that you begin being our captains here, and first get us the pay from Seuthes whether he will or no, but don't take us away before."

Polycrates the Athenian said (prompted by Xenophon), "Why, man," says he, "I see Heracleides here too! That man was entrusted with the property which we won by hard work, and he sold it, and did not give the proceeds either to Seuthes or to us. He stole it and keeps it himself! Let's get hold of him, if we have any sense; for this fellow," says he, "is not a Thracian, he's a Hellene and he cheats his own countrymen!"

When Heracleides heard this, he was dismayed; he found Seuthes, and said, "Let's get out of the claws of these men, if we are wise." They jumped on their horses and galloped away to their own camp. Then Seuthes sent Abrozelmes, his own interpreter, to Xenophon, and asked him to stay behind with a thousand men-at-arms, and promised to give him the forts by the sea and others besides. Then he told him as a secret, which he had heard from Polynicos, that if he came into the hands of the Lacedaimonians Thibron certainly meant to put him to death. Many others sent similar messages to Xenophon, and they warned him he was calumniated and he must look out. On hearing all this he took two victims and sacrificed to Zeus the King, asking whether it was better to stay with Seuthes on the terms he offered, or to leave along with the army. The answer was to leave.

VII

After that Seuthes went farther away and encamped; the Hellenes took up quarters in the villages where they could collect as much food as possible before they went down to the sea. These villages had been given by Seuthes to Menosades, and Menosades was indignant when he saw his property being used up there. So, taking with him Odryses, a very powerful chief of those who had come down from inland, and about thirty horsemen, he came to the Hellenic camp and called Xenophon outside. Xenophon came to meet him with some of his officers and friends, and Menosades said, "I protest against this pillaging of our villages. I speak for Seuthes, and this man has come from Medocos who is king inland, and we demand that you leave the country; otherwise we will not put up with it, but we will resist you as enemies if you ravage our country."

Xenophon answered. "You are the last man who ought to speak so, and it is not easy to answer you: but for the sake of this young man I will tell him about us both, and he may compare us. Before we became your friends," he said, "we marched where we would through this country, plundering and burning at will; and when you came to us on embassy, you lodged beside us fearing no enemy. Your people hardly came into the country at all, or if you did, you lodged as in an enemy country, with your horses bitted and bridled. Then you became our friends, and through us you hold the land by God's help; and now see how you drive us from this land, which we gained by force of arms and handed over to you! For as you know, the enemy were not able to drive us out. You gave us no gifts and no help; it is no return for service which you claim now you send us away; far from it—we are on the way out already, and so far as possible you will not let us even camp in the country. When you make this demand you have no shame before heaven, or before this man; although he sees you now rich, whereas you lived on pillage before you became our friend, as you said yourself. And then what's the use of addressing me?" says he; "I am no longer in command, but the Lacedaimonians, to whom you have passed over that army to take away—without consulting me, if you please! I came into their bad graces by bringing the army to you, and you would not give me the chance of doing them a good turn by passing them on!"

When Odryses heard this he said, "I'm ready to sink into the earth with shame, Medosades, when I hear such things! If I had known before, I would never have come with you;

and now I depart. King Medocos would not be pleased either, if I should drive out a benefactor." With these words he got on his horse and rode off with the other horsemen, all but four or five.

Medosades was still angry at the plundering, and told Xenophon to summon the two Laconians. He approached them in company with the best men he had, and told them that Medosades summoned them, and what his demand was that they should leave the country. "I believe then," he said, "that you will get the money due, if you say they have asked you to demand their pay from Seuthes, whether he likes it or not, and that they will follow you gladly if they get that; that you have promised the soldiers to go at once when they have their rights."

The Laconians agreed; they would say this and more as forcibly as they could, and they set out at once, taking with them the most suitable persons. When they arrived Charminos said:

"Have you anything to say to us, Medosades? If not, we have something to say to you." Medosades answered very submissively, "I have to say this, and Seuthes the same: we expect not to be injured by you now that we have become friends. For if you injure these people, you injure us; they are our people." Then the Laconians answered, "Well, we are ready to go as soon as the men receive the pay which they demand from you. If not, we are coming to defend them now, and to punish certain persons who have broken their oaths and wronged them. If you are really such, we shall begin to gain our rights from you." And Xenophon said, "Would you be content, Medosades, to leave it to these people in whose country we are, your friends as you call them? Let them decide by vote whether you should leave the country or we?" He said No to that; but he said the best thing would be for the two Laconians to approach Seuthes about the pay, and he thought Seuthes would agree.

The next thing was to send Xenophon with him, and he promised to demand it. He only asked them not to burn the villages.

Then they sent Xenophon with the men who seemed best, and he said to Seuthes:

"I come to claim nothing, Seuthes; but to show that you were not right to be angry with me, because I claimed so urgently from you what you had promised for the soldiers. In fact, I thought it no less useful for yourself than for them. First, I believed that after heaven it was they had made you famous; they made you king of a great country and a great population, so that nothing you do can be hidden, whether good or bad. For such a man it seemed a great thing not to be thought so ungrateful as to dismiss his benefactors; and a great thing to have a good name with six thousand men; but greatest of all not to make yourself distrusted when you make a promise. Indeed, I see that when men are distrusted, their words are blown about empty and ineffective and despised; but whenever men are known to keep their word, if they want anything their words have no less power than the force of others: and if they desire to make people reasonable, I perceive that their threats bring them to reason no less than summary punishment from others. And if such men make a promise, they achieve no less than others do by a gift on the spot. Just remember yourself what you paid in advance when you took us as allies. Nothing!—you know it. But we believed what you said would be made true, when you encouraged all these men to join your army, and to win you a domain worth no less than thirty talents, the sum which these men claim, many times more indeed. Then the belief and trust, which won your empire, is being sold only for the money we claim.

"Remember again, how great a prize you thought the conquest which you have made. I am well assured that you would rather have achieved what you have achieved than to receive many times as much as our claim. I believe myself that it would be a heavier blow, and more discreditable, not to keep now what you have than not to get it then; just as it is harder to become poor after being rich than never to have been rich at all, more painful to become nobody after being king than never to have been king at all.

"You know also that those who have become your subjects were not persuaded by friendship to be ruled by you, but yielded to necessity, and they would try to make themselves free again unless fear restrained them. Then what do you think would make them fear you more and behave reasonably? If they should see the soldiers so disposed to you that they would stand by if you told them, and come back at once if you needed them, and if others heard from them such good stories about you that they would join you whenever you wished? Or if they should suspect that no-one else would ever come to you because these doings made them distrust your word, and even your own men felt much inclined to this same feeling? Really and truly, these people yielded to you from no lack of numbers, but only from lack of leaders. Then there's a risk now that they may find leaders in some of those who think you have wronged them, or even in the Lacedaimonians who are stronger still: suppose the soldiers promise more willing service to them if they exact what is due from you, and if the Lacedaimonians agree because they want the army! Besides, it is plain enough that the Thracians who are now under your rule would be readier to march against you than with you; for under your rule slavery is their lot; if you were conquered it would be freedom.

"Again, if you think you must care for the country now as being your own, how do you think it more likely to be uninjured? Suppose these men receive what they claim; they would depart and leave peace behind them. But suppose they remain in the country as enemies, and you should try to bring in as many again and more to fight on your side, all wanting provisions! And which would cost you most money—if you pay what is due to these, or if you have to pay others, a force strong enough to conquer them, and leave the debt still due? Heracleides, indeed, as he used to explain to me, found the sum enormous. Well, I declare it is much less now for you to get and to give than it was then to pay the tenth part before we came. For no fixt limit divides much and little, but only how much one can give and the other can take. And now your yearly income will be more than your whole possessions then.

"All I have said, Seuthes, has been forethought for a friend; I wished you to be thought worthy of the goods which the gods have given you; and also that my name should not be ruined in the army. For I assure you that I could do nothing in the army now, whether I wished to injure an enemy or to help you again. That is how they are disposed towards me. But I protest before the gods, who know, and before you, that I have never received anything from you on account of the soldiers, and I have never asked you for what is theirs, and indeed never asked you to give me what you promised: if you had offered it, on my oath I never would have taken it, unless the soldiers were to receive their own also. It would have been a disgrace to make sure of mine, and to look on while they were wronged, especially as they held me in honour. Of course Heracleides thinks everything is rubbish compared with money, wholly and absolutely; but my opinion is, Seuthes, that a man can have no finer or more glorious possession, especially a ruler, than virtue and justice and generosity. For who has these is rich: friends are his wealth, those many he has and the many who wish to be; while he prospers, many are glad with him, and if he comes to grief, he lacks not those who will help.

"However, if you have not found out from my actions that I was heart and soul your friend, and if you cannot learn this from these words of mine, at least take notice of the words of all the soldiers: you were there yourself, and you heard what they said, wishing to find fault with me. They accused me to the Lacedaimonians that I rated you higher than the Lacedaimonians, and their private charge was that I cared more for your interests than theirs; they also said I had received gifts from you. What do you think: did they see any ill will in me towards you when they accuse me of receiving gifts from you? Had they not noticed my great readiness to serve you? I really think all the world believe that one ought to show goodwill to one who presents him with gifts. And what of you? Before I had served you in any way you received me pleasantly with eyes and voice, you entertained me, and made promises for the future— which have not been fulfilled; and when you had done what you wished, and now that you have become very great, and I did my best, now the soldiers dishonour me, and you can endure to look on! No, I believe you will decide to pay this money; time will be your teacher, and you will never allow yourself to see your benefactors accusing you. Therefore I beg you, when you do pay, that you will take care to leave me as you found me with the soldiers."

After hearing this Seuthes cursed the man who was the cause why this pay had not been given long ago; all suspected this to be Heracleides. "I myself," says he, "never had a notion to cheat you, and pay I will!" Then Xenophon said again, "Since you mean to pay, now I beg you to pay through me! Don't allow me to stand differently in the army now from the time when we came to you." He said, "No! you shall not be less in honour with the army for my sake; and if you will stay with me, bringing only a thousand men-at-arms, I will give you those forts and all else that I promised!" Xenophon said, "To do that is quite impossible; just let us go." "Why, look," said Seuthes, "you will be safer here with me." Xenophon said again, "Many thanks for your goodwill, but for me, to stay is impossible. Yet when I shall be in better honour, believe that this will be a blessing for you also." Then Seuthes said, "Money I have only a little here, and that I give you, a talent; but oxen six hundred, and sheep about four thousand, and captives a hundred and fifty or so. Take these, and take those who cheated you as hostages, and then you may go." Xenophon laughed, and said, "Well, if this does not come up to the pay, whose talent shall I say this is? There's danger for me, and I had better look out for stones; you heard the threats." For the time he stayed there.

Next day Seuthes gave over what he had promised, and sent drovers with them. The soldiers had been saying that Xenophon intended to make a home with Seuthes and to get what he had been promised; but as soon as they saw him, they ran up to him with joy. Xenophon saw Charminos and Polynicos, and said to them, "Because of you, all this has been kept safe for the army, and here I give it to you; pray arrange to distribute it to the men." So they took it over, and appointed spoil-sellers and sold it, and the men were very much discontented. Xenophon took no part; he was clearly preparing for his homeward journey, for this was before the sentence of his banishment had been given in Athens. But the authorities in the army came and begged him not to leave until he should lead them to Thibron and hand over the army to him.

VIII

After that they sailed across to Lampsacos, and there Xenophon was met by Eucleides, a Phleiasian seer, the son of Cleagoras, who painted the frescoes in the Lyceion. This man congratulated Xenophon on being safe and sound, and asked how much gold he had. Xenophon said on his oath that there would not be enough to pay his way home, unless he could sell his horse and what he had about him. The man would not believe. The Lampsacenes sent him gifts of friendship, and while he was sacrificing to Apollo, he asked Eucleides to be there; then Eucleides at the sacrifice said he believed now that Xenophon had no money. "But I'm sure," says he, "that even if you are going to get some an obstacle comes in the way; if no other, you are your own obstacle!" Xenophon agreed. The man said, "Yes, the obstacle is Zeus Merciful;" and he asked, "Have you sacrificed already, as I used to do at home for you, with whole burnt-offering?" Xenophon replied that he had never sacrificed to that god since his travels began. So the man advised him to do as he used to do; said things would be better that way.

Next day Xenophon went to Ophrynion and sacrificed a whole burnt-offering of pigs in the family fashion, and the omens were good. On this day arrived Bion and Nausicleides with pay for the army; they were entertained by Xenophon and they brought back his horse, which he had sold in Lampsacos for fifty darics; they suspected he had sold it for want of money, because they had heard how he loved that horse, so they gave it back and would not let him return the price.

After that they marched through the Troad, and crossing Ida, they reached Antandros, then sailed by sea to the plain of Thebe. From that place they made their way through Adramyttion and Certonos to the plain of the Caïcos, and so reached Pergamos in Mysia.

Then Xenophon was entertained by Hellas, the wife of Gongylos the Eretrian. She informed him that there was a Persian Asidates in that plain; she said he could capture him with wife and children and cattle, numbers of cattle, if he attacked at night with three hundred men. She sent to show them the way her own cousin, and Daphnagoras,

one whom she valued very highly. So Xenophon, keeping
these two with him, sacrificed. Basias the Elean seer was
present, and said the omens were most favourable, and
the man could be taken. After supper, then, he set out,
taking with him the officers who had been most friendly
and faithful to him all through, in hopes to do them a good
turn. Others came thrusting themselves in to join, but the
officers refused. "We don't want them to have a share," they
said, as if the spoil was in their hands.

They arrived about midnight, but they neglected captives and cattle around the tower, and most of them escaped,
for they wanted to capture the man himself and his belong-
ings. They attacked the tower, but failed to storm it, for
it was very tall and large, had bulwarks and strong men to
defend it. So they began to dig through the wall. It was
eight clay bricks in thickness, but by daybreak the light
showed through; at the first glimpse of light someone
struck through with an iron rod large enough to spit a
whole ox, and ran through the thigh of the nearest man.
After that they shot arrows through the hole, so that it was
not safe to come anywhere near the place. Then with shouting and beacon-fires they brought help, Itamenes and his
force, and from Comania Assyrian men-at-arms and Hyr-
canian horsemen, about eighty, who were also in the king's
pay, and others, light-armed troops, about eight hundred,
others from Parthenion, others from Apollonia and from the
neighbouring villages, and horsemen also.

Then it was high time to look for a way of retreat. They
took all the cattle and sheep and captives and made a square
with these in the middle; they were not anxious about the
booty so much as fearful that the retreat might become a
scampering if they left the booty behind, and if the enemy
should be bold and the soldiers discouraged—but now they
retreated ready to fight for their winnings. When Gongylos
saw how few the Hellenes were, and how many the enemy,
he sallied out himself against his mother's wish with his own

force, eager to take a part; other supports were Procles from Halisarna, and Teuthranias, who was descended from Damaratos. Xenophon's party were very hard pressed by this time with arrows and slingstones, and marched in a ring, to keep their shields in front of the arrows; it was all they could do to cross the River Carcasos, and almost half of them were wounded. There Agasias, the Stymphalian lieutenant, was wounded; he had been fighting the whole time. They came in safe at last with about two hundred captives, and sheep enough for sacrifices.

Next day Xenophon sacrificed, and led out the whole army by night. He intended to take the most roundabout way through Lydia, to put the people off their guard; he hoped they might not be alarmed by thinking he was near. Asidates heard that Xenophon had sacrificed for another attack on himself, and was out with all the army, and he quartered himself in some villages under the town of Parthenion. There Xenophon and his force came upon him, and captured him and his wife and children, and the horses and all he had; so the first omens came true. Then they returned to Pergamos. There Xenophon gave hearty thanks to God: for all joined together, the Laconians and the other captains and the under-officers and the soldiers, and gave him the choice of horses and oxen and everything; so he was now well able to do a good turn to another.

Then Thibron arrived and took over the army, which he mingled with the rest of the Hellenic forces, and marched to the war against Tissaphernes and Pharnabazos.

NOTE BY AN ANCIENT EDITOR

The distance of the whole journey, up country and down country, was 215 stages, 1,150 leagues, 34,255 stades, or about 3,360 geographic miles.

The time taken was one year and three months.

Ann Arbor Paperbacks